Gerda Van de Perd.

GEERTJE

GEERTJE

War Seen through the Eyes of a Child as an Adult

GERDA BLOKHUIS VANDENHAAK

Geertje

iUniverse books may be ordered through booksellers or by contacting:

iUniverse
1663 Liberty Drive
Bloomington, IN 47403
www.iuniverse.com
1-800-Authors (1-800-288-4677)

Because of the dynamic nature of the Internet, any web addresses or links contained in this book may have changed since publication and may no longer be valid. The views expressed in this work are solely those of the author and do not necessarily reflect the views of the publisher, and the publisher hereby disclaims any responsibility for them.

Any people depicted in stock imagery provided by Thinkstock are models, and such images are being used for illustrative purposes only. Certain stock imagery © Thinkstock.

ISBN: 978-1-4917-8551-5 (sc)
ISBN: 978-1-4917-9010-6 (e)

Library of Congress Control Number: 2016907043

Print information available on the last page.

iUniverse rev. date: 04/29/2016

This book is dedicated with love to my
children and grandchildren,
in memory of my dear daughter, Peggy Barendregt,
and beloved husband, Andrew Vandenhaak.

Contents

Introduction & Acknowledgements

This book has been a long time in the making. As the second child of nine, I used to always make up stories to tell to my siblings at bedtime. Children's story books were rare and costly, so I made up my own. I always wanted to write, but received no encouragement in the school I attended. When it came to writing, I always got a failing mark. I did continue writing, but always destroyed whatever I wrote. Yet I felt this need to write; to write about my experiences and what I observed around me.

I am a 77-year-old mother of 5 and grandmother of 23. I live in Alberta Canada and I volunteer as a facilitator for Darkness to Light's *Stewards of Children* Program (www.d2L.org). Since September 2000, I have trained 1290 people in the prevention of sexual abuse of children. In 2010, I became a recipient of the Global TV's *Woman of Vision* Award.

Twelve years ago, I was told that journaling was a healthy way to heal from all that bothered you. I tried to think as far back into my life as I could; tried to feel back the feelings I felt then. I was born in Holland, on Dec 29, 1937. This was two years before WWII. I do vaguely remember fleeing for the first time in 1940 and being on a boat, sitting on Grandma's lap, but nothing more. No clear picture came. Then suddenly the war memories came flooding back. I do not know if they all are accurate, but they truly are my memories. I now smile at that little girl. She was so scared but proud at the same time; convinced at that her meager food gathering efforts kept the family alive. From there, the war stories were born. Since then, I have kept my stories and I also began to write poems. Those I also kept. I even ventured out and would sometimes post a poem or story on Facebook. I was pleasantly surprised with the response. For the first time in my life, I received compliments on my stories and poems. Is this for real? Can I write after all? My confidence was building.

Amongst all of this came the diagnosis of my late husband's cancer and his passing away. When I looked at my children and grandchildren, I wanted to leave something of him and of myself for them. I wanted them to truly "know" us. And so, I gathered my stories and poems and decided to put them all in a book. Sometimes it seemed like a foolish dream, other times I was filled with determination. It was a long and tough journey but I made it. The book is finished.

A special thanks to my encouragers: Arlene Verhelst, Chantelle Vanderveen, Darlene Dykstra, Hetty Jagersma, and Rachel Breukelman. Thank you for pushing and pummeling me along the road to publishing this book. Without your support, I am not sure I would have come this far.

I also would like to thank my beloved granddaughters, Bridgette Vandenhaak and Kailyn Leffers, the illustrators of this book.

Gerda Vandenhaak nee Blokhuis.

Through the Eyes of a Child

The Netherlands, World War II

I am lining up for food. I can feel the crackling of the papers my mom put under my jacket, against the wind. I have in my hands a round, brown enamel, little pan with two black handles. The edge is black too and there is a chip broken off the edge. We line up at the soup kitchen. I see no adults. It must be for children only. But I do not see my brother and sister. The soup smells good. It is grayish brown. It makes me feel good inside.

I keep looking at my legs. They feel so heavy. I am surprised every time I look at them. They look the same. It seems like I am wading through something heavy. I don't know why I feel that way. I did not find much food today, only a white paper bag with some powder in it. I don't know what it is. I did not even steal it. I found it on a windowsill. When I walk into the house, mom right away puts her arms around me and says: "What's the matter?" Nothing is the matter. I only have this powder and I hand it to mom. Mom smiles and seems to be happy with it. "Salt," she said "Real salt, this is great!" She pulls me towards her and holds me and then I tell her about the dead people and the three that we knew. Mom cries and I let her. "Are you sure?" she asked. "Yes, I checked," I tell her. Then my mom holds me so tight, it almost hurts, but it also makes me feel good. Mom says it is a good thing that they do not shoot children, so I won't tell her about the twins.

My brother and I are standing outside in the darkness. Our backs are pressed against the wall of our house. I am seven and my brother is five years old. I can feel the roughness of the wall under my left hand. My brother is very brave. He holds my hand very tightly. I am never afraid. My mother told us to wait before we start walking; to wait until we can see. And if we were afraid, she told us to look up to the stars and God would look after us. We have to get some milk for the baby. Mom only has water for her. We have to go to the second farm. Mom said not to go to the first one. We walk slowly; we do not talk, not even whisper. People are not allowed to be outside after eight. We come to the farm and knock on the back door. It opens and a hand pulls us inside. The door is closed behind us and then a candle is lit. The warmth of the place puts its arms around us. "What do you want? You are only kids," a voice said. We ask for some milk for the baby. The farmer's wife smiles at us and said "Yes." I can feel my insides again. The farmer's wife said we could come again as she fills the milk container. When we got home, mom hugged us so tight, it almost hurt again. Mom loves us so much.

I did it! All morning I had waited on the side of the road with the other kids for the trucks with the sugar beets to come by. We waited at the place where the trucks really slowed down because of the curve. I jumped on the back of the truck and now had three sugar beets: two I grabbed and one that fell down after me. My arm was scraped and blood trickled down one leg, but I did not feel it at all. I was so overjoyed with the beets that I ran all the way home. My brother and I cleaned the beets in the kitchen sink and then we sucked on them. I can still taste and feel the breaking of the beet skin. It felt funny. For the next two days we sucked the beets. At night we would climb in mom and dad's bed and huddle together under the blankets. I don't remember what happened after that. But I do know that that was the last time I needed to steal food.

I sit between them, my mother and her friend. We are riding the horse and buggy to the concentration camp in Amersfoort to visit Dad and the friend's husband. The buggy belongs to the friend. We have two plates of food wrapped in towels in the back. They talk softly right above my head. I can hear every word. The steady talking makes me sleepy. I am so hungry and now we are bringing food to the camp. Why? We need food ourselves! Suddenly we are there. I even see my dad. He is wearing pajamas. Strange. Mom's friend talks to the guard. The guard shakes his head. Mom starts to cry, so the guard does not look at her again. We go to the fence. The men all look funny, as if they are dead. I have seen dead men. These men look the same but still walk. The guard starts yelling and the men leave, including my dad. He looks at us. His eyes are very strange. Then he leaves too. We go back home. In the back are two plates of food. Mashed potatoes with red cabbage. Mom says we can share it when we get back home. I want to eat it so badly, but I keep thinking of my dad and I feel bad about wanting the food. I don't want to feel anymore.

I am setting the table in the dining room. Mom is singing in the kitchen and that makes all of us happy. She got a whole whack of potato peels and she washed them and washed them. Now they are cooked and she added some red cabbage. Yummy. It smells good and we are getting a meal today. It is my brother's turn to sit in dad's chair today. As usual, I open my eyes really quick, just for a second, while mom prays. I am sure that when mom prays, that God, Jesus and the angels are there in the dining room with us. But again I was not quick enough. We start to eat. Then suddenly sirens, shooting and yelling. We all jump up and run to our hiding places under our house. There are three different hiding places. I know that but mom does not know that I know that. I have taken my plate of food with me and go to the farthest corner of the place, my little brother next to me. Other people are coming in and find a place to sit. I hold my plate close to me, my arms protective above it. Someone sees my plate of food and wants to take it away. I started to cry and suddenly there is my mom. She says: "This is still my house and this is my daughter. This is her food and she is going to eat it." My mom sits next to me and I still feel her arm around me as I eat. I just could not stop crying and my sobs fill the room. People are telling me to be quiet, but I just can't. I eat and I sob and sob. Even when I was quiet, my body kept shaking. All night my mother kept her arm around me. My big sister was on the one side and me on the other, my brother next to me. I did not care about all the other people, just about us and my mom. All night long there was yelling and loud noises around us and all night long mom prayed. First out loud with all the people and then softly just with us.

Mom woke us up and told us to get ready quick. "Dad is home," she said, "and we have to flee." In minutes we were on the road running. Mom is pushing the baby buggy. In the middle of the night we are running. I am confused. There is shooting and yelling again and the piercing scream of some missile. I am terribly afraid. We wind up in the middle of a skirmish near Nykerk. A soldier came and told dad to go the other way and so we did. I remember falling asleep under a bridge and then waking up in the morning in the middle of a field with dads arms around the three of us. We started walking again. This time down a path at the bottom of the dike. Mom was pushing the buggy. In it was the baby and a little pan of cooked horsemeat, taken from a dead horse behind our house. Dad found a bicycle. He walked alongside it while pushing my oldest sister who was sitting on the crossbar. My brother was walking in front of me, step by step. His feet were bleeding. We walked on, all alone, in the country side. Late in the afternoon we rounded a curve in the dike and we saw a farmhouse. I can still see it. It had orange ribbons all over it and a sign that said they were *free*! We did it! We somehow had broken through and were free! I really did not know what that meant. The farmers welcomed us and took us into their home. The farmer's wife set us all up at the table and gave us a bowl of hot oatmeal with milk and some brown powder. Brown sugar she called it. Dad prayed with us. His voice again sounded funny and mom cried. It was the most wonderful meal I had ever tasted. We all sat there and smiled at each other and cried some more. Dad said we were free and the war was over. We would never be hungry again. The next day we reached our destination, Putten.

Hiding Places

The war is over. Things are returning to normal. I hear this all the time. What is normal? There has always been war. It is all I can remember. The first time we had to flee I was only two years and four months old. I was sitting on my grandma's lap and she was sitting on a roll of ropes with her back against the mast. Someone was sick in a blue potty. Mom was holding my little brother. Was that normal? That is as far as I can think back.

I do not understand the way we have to live now. I have to go to school? Why? I am now seven years old. I have never been to school. Mom has taught me to read and write. I can read any book I want. I can also add and subtract, so what else do I need? They all make me so busy; I have no time to think. I have to think about things. But I need time for that. And I have no time of my own. We now have a family with 5 kids living with us. We had to take them in because their house is gone. While people are rebuilding, we must all live in the homes that survived. I do not like those people. They take up three rooms and we have to share the bathroom with them. I am angry.

We all have to bring a piece of firewood along with us to school. That is to keep the school warm. No wood, no school. Some of the kids throw their piece of wood in the harbor, that way they can play hooky. I throw my wood in the water. I am the last one. The first bell rings. Everyone runs off to school and I hide under the bridge. I sit there all alone. My back against the cement wall. My knees up under my chin. My arms wrapped around my knees. This is my hiding place. The place where I can be just me. The place where I can think. The place where I can look at all things and examine them and put them away. I can listen to words my Mom used and think about them. I can hear my Dad's prayers and wonder about heaven and about God.

Then I go to my fairy tale. I spin on it every chance I get. I walk in a garden with all the princes and princesses. Lots of flowers and birds. The music is soft and ever so gentle. It holds me. I listen to the music and smell the sweetness of the flowers. I sit there until I am all still and happy inside.

At twelve noon, I hear the kids run across the bridge to go home to eat lunch. I rejoin them and simply go to school in the afternoon.

I would not have made it through that first year would I have been without my hiding place.

I have thrown myself across the bed. I am *not* crying. My hand keeps touching my cheek. It hurts. It *really* hurts. *Mom hit me.* She hit me hard with the back of her hand, right across the face. I just don't understand anything anymore. I used to do things right, now all I do is wrong!

I am very good at 'grab and run'. It was a head of lettuce and a cucumber today. Mom took it scolded me and took it back to the man. Why? I desperately try to find my hiding place, but today, I just can't. I feel so cold inside. *My Mom hit me*! She has *never* hit me before. Why is bringing food home suddenly wrong?

Mom comes into our room. She strokes my hair and asks me to sit up. She has been crying too. She tries to explain again, but I just don't get it. Why is stealing suddenly wrong? Now she tells me it was always wrong? I look at mom and I no longer hear the words. Words keep coming out of her mouth. I see that mom has a line right across her forehead. I never noticed she had big ears before. The words continue to come. I just let them fall. I hear them but they no longer connect. Mom's eyes are brown and I see green and golden flecks in them. She now shakes my shoulders and asks me something. What? Oh, I have to promise something: never to take anything without paying for it. Okay, have it your way. "I promise!" Mom's words still come. They float all over my room, some I catch, some escape, and some are like music, but they will not go inside of me. For a long time, I lay still on my bed. Not thinking, not feeling. Just being in nothingness. Until my brother comes to call me. It is time to eat.

War is Abusive

When I read my "war" stories a couple of weeks after I wrote them and discovered they all had to do with food, it was a big eye opener. One other thing that struck me was that I had decided to not feel anymore because feeling simply *hurts*.

As a child I saw too much. Yesterday was reminder of that. A reminder that although it has been 70 years since World War II officially ended, for some of us it *never* ended.

The hunger and fear were the worst. Somehow I still think that is what affected me the most, for that is what comes back all the time. As an objective person now, I think was it really? Why not the killing of people, the murder of the two little boys, the dead eyes of the men and my father in the concentration camp, the blood running from the girl who I thought was dead, but was not? Why are they not the first things that assault me? Why is the first thing for me the fear and the smell of fear?

I know that as a child I first retreated to my hiding place. A place where I did not have to feel. I did not have to care. A place where I could watch myself, see myself steal food and be safe, for I was watching over me. Telling myself how to do it. How to be the first and the fastest. But it was not me doing it. And yet, it worked! I always managed to get some food for the family. At age seven, I was the provider. I was very proud of that fact. Immensely proud. I had found my purpose in life. I provided food for the family, so no one would die. We survived!

Aftermath

About thirty-five years ago, I got a call from a friend. She had people over from Holland and they came from the same town as we did. My friend asked if they could come for coffee? "No problem," I said. They arrived while I was in the bedroom. Andy opened the door and greeted them. I heard them speak and suddenly I heard a voice from the past. 'The man' spoke and I instantly headed for the bathroom and puked my guts out. Andy came to call me and saw how sick I was. I could hear them talk and talk. And I just stayed in my bedroom with frequent dashes to the bathroom. My fear and panic was that great! I absolutely did not understand why. I kept thinking about and seeing a bicycle. I did not know why. I was working with two different girls at that time. Both of them had been sexually abused and I suddenly realized that I had the same symptoms. I tried to explore that notion for a while, but came up with nothing.

At that time the movie *The Holocaust* was being shown on TV. We had no TV, so we watched it at a friend's house. We only saw the first part. We could not sleep, both had nightmares and flashbacks and my first story was 'born'.

Sometime during the last 6 months of the war years, I wound up living with another family. I did not know where my parents or siblings had gone too. I think dad was in the camp and mom in the hospital, she took the baby with her. I do remember visiting her and she was in a bed outside of the hospital building.

The family I lived with lived in the country. I could not see any other homes from their place. They lived in a duplex on some sort of hobby farm. In the other half of the duplex lived 'the man' with his wife and baby. Several times during my stay, he would offer to take me for a bike ride. "I will take her out of your hair for an hour or so," he would say and I wondered what he was talking about.

I loved the bike rides. We would go quite far. I would sit on the bar up in the front, no bike seat. The wind would blow in my face and I felt so free as if we were flying. After a while we would come up on a little shed in the field. A shelter for the rain. We would go in and see about six or eight other men there. All German soldiers. They were nice. They gave me sausages and chocolate. They also always told me not to tell anyone about this. Of course, I would not tell anyone. You think I was nuts? Telling others about this food? No way! I even made sure it was all wiped off my lips when we left for home. 'The man' would talk to the soldiers. They would talk about names and addresses. I did not know what it was all about. I got good food and was content.

After the war was over, I had to go to the police station with my mom. She told me not to be afraid and just answer the questions. There were two police officers and a lady. She did not say a thing, she was just writing. They asked me about 'the man' and the bike rides. About where we went on our bike rides and if we talked to anyone. It scared me. I did know how to keep secrets, but not how to tell them. I felt guilty. Mom said it was okay to talk and tell them. So I did. I told them all about the shed and the soldiers, about the sausages and the chocolate. They asked what 'the man' talked about. I told them I did not know, it was just names and addresses. I had to tell them that three times and it made me cry. Mom told them to stop it. On the way back home, she told me I did really well and she was proud of me.

I know now that 'the man' was an NSB. A spy. A person who reported the people who were hiding the Jewish people. They also report the names of the other people in hiding and the members of the KP. He went to jail for a long time.

I know I was a child. I know I am not responsible or at fault but yet I feel the guilt. I did not understand what was going on in that shed, but if I had told someone about the sausages and chocolate, he would have been found out and lives would have been saved. But the food, it meant so much to me. I am not apologizing, or maybe I am. I am just explaining, or journaling. I am not sure. I feel so utterly bad about this.

Finding Me

In the late fifties, a lot of young people traveled all over to 'find' themselves. I was one of them. I was very shy; afraid of groups and liked to stay by myself but yet hated it at the same time. When I did go anywhere, I put my all over mask on. This time I was travelling through Europe. I got myself a motorbike, leathers and a pup tent. I strapped my guitar on the back of my bike and off I went. People do not bother bikers, unless they want to be bothered. So this rough and tough looking girl went to every museum and into old buildings and twelve-hundred-year-old Churches and many more things like that. I stood in awe of the masters and architects of the past.

One day as I am riding through a forest, I come to a still place. That is the only way I could describe it. It was a gloomy day. The still place was in a clearing. Railroad tracks ran through the middle and came to a sudden stop in a pile of gravel. A lonely bench stood on one side. I stopped my bike and looked at the gravel. The stones were all smooth and round: small ones and larger ones all of different colors. I picked up two smooth stones and put them in my pocket and left, but not before picking up a brochure that was available for passersby. I did not look at the brochure until two days later. All the while, my hands played with the stones in my pocket. Then when I needed to make a fire and was looking for some paper, I found the brochure back and sat down and read it. It told the story of the Jewish people that had been taken to this place to board the train, never to be seen again. The place had been kept as a memorial and every smooth stone represented a life that had once been. My hands were holding two stones that I had removed from the memorial. Two lives. I could not forget this, no matter how hard I tried. So I turned back. I found the place again. This time it was a beautiful afternoon. The sun was shining through the trees. The sunlight filtered on my hands as I sat on the bench holding the stones and crying for no reason. I carefully put the stones back and prayed. I knew I was in a special and holy place. I asked my Father in Heaven to help me and guide me in all of life. Sometimes I am still looking to 'find' me but I also know that my God had found me.

Forgive Me!

The waiting room was full. I pulled number 135. I just knew it would be a long wait. I sat down next to a nondescript woman. Everything about her was a brownish grey. One look around and I knew most of us were here to get our pension applications in. Everyone was around the same age: sixty-five. I took out my papers and gave them a quick glance over. Everything was there.

The woman next to me then asked me, "Can you look at mine?"

I felt instant resentment boiling up. Why did people not make sure they had everything in order before they showed up? But yet, I said:" Okay, let's look." I saw her name, date of birth and nationality; German. I thought nothing of it. When I started asking questions while going through her papers, she noticed my Dutch accent.

"Forgive me!" she suddenly said.

I looked up, surprised and asked, "What?"

"Forgive me for what we did during the war."

"The war? You were just a child, just like me. You did nothing wrong."

Then she told me. She told me about the war and how they had to go to school and salute the hated flag. It was a Lutheran village and most of the kids did not salute the flag. Their parents told them it was wrong, she did not understand why. She was only eight-years-old. One morning soldiers came in black uniforms and told the kids that if they did not salute the flag they would be shot. The little girl in front of her did not salute. She was shot! She told me about how scared she was and that she *saluted* the flag. She was crying now. People were looking at us. Her sobs were loud.

Again she lifted her tear streaked face to me and said: "Forgive me!"

"You were just a child" I said again. We were standing now, facing each other, no longer aware of the others in the room.

"Please, please, just one time in my life I want to hear someone say 'I forgive you'," she cried.

I did it, I said, "I forgive you!"

We stood there oblivious to all others. We hugged each other and both cried. We cried for the sorrow and the abuse of war. The sorrow we both had gone through. The hunger, the pain and the fear.

Calling number 135.

Meltdown

Hmm. How to start. I have a terrible fear of heights. But that does not mean I have to be in a high place to get an attack. Now picture me walking down the sidewalk, fit to kill, carrying a briefcase filled with papers for a court appearance. One of my clients has been charged with tax evasion. My mind is on that and what I should say. As I am walking down the street, I glance up and it happens. A window cleaner is washing the windows on a high-rise office building. The next moment my briefcase goes flying. I am sitting on the sidewalk crying and blubbering and speaking in tongues. At least no one can understand me. People pat my back and want to call the ambulance. A little boy asks his mama, "Is that a crazy lady?" I now have my head between my legs and am taking deep breaths. A cop wants to know what I have been taking. All I want is my briefcase, a glass of water, and a deep hole to crawl in. I love an audience, but not while I am sitting on my butt on a sidewalk and crying.

Adrian

November 21st, 1969 was the day that the Lord blessed us with a little miracle. Right from his birth his life was in danger. Our doctor had just read about the Isolette, but the hospital did not have one, so he made his own. An aquarium was used, so no holes on the side. He fabricated a light above it from an old light found in the basement of the hospital. A fluorescent light. What a contraption. Our boy could not drink, cry, or retain body heat and a host of other things. He needed blood transfusions, but his blood type was not available. Every day he became weaker. He was receiving IV therapy and kept losing weight. We did not dare sleep, for we were sure we would lose him if we did.

Day six came and he suddenly cried for the first time! We rejoiced at this small, to us, victory. We cried. We prayed and we hoped for a miracle. Still no blood available. On day eight we learned that all of his organs were now affected. We were asked permission to turn off the machine that kept him alive. We unanimously said, "No!" They told us he would never be more than a vegetable; he would be very handicapped and did not have the brains to suck from a bottle. We continued to say, "No". I had my running conversations with God.

Day ten and we had to name him. Andy had just left, so I called him Adrian, after his father, for I always liked his real name better then Andrew. His middle name is Paul after the three girls who shared a room with me; they all had a son and they all called their sons Paul. Those girls helped me through. They listened and prayed with me.

Since birth, we could only look at him through a window. My whole body longed to hold him. To touch him. To caress him. We were told to call the Minister, so he could come and Baptize him. We knew so very surely that Baptism would not make any difference at all; he was a child of God.

Day eleven would have been his final day but God sent a miracle. Blood! Blood that he needed. Blood that would by the grace of God save him.

We sat in the hallway of the hospital. It was three o'clock in the morning and we were praying and crying and hoping against hope. The elevator door opened and our doctor walked out holding a baby. A strange new baby. He did not look like ours. This one was pink, not yellow. This one was moving, kicking and crying. The doctor handed him to us and walked away after saying, "It is about time that you spend some time with your son." Yes, he, the doctor, was crying, just like us. We saw a nurse in the hallway, also crying. Tears of happiness. Of relief. Of thankfulness. Praise be to God.

We were told he did not have the brains to suck and would not be more than a vegetable. For the next twelve years I argued with GOD. He gave me this child and I wanted him to live! For the first ten years we took him weekly to the hospital for his blood tests. I prayed constantly and demanded that God would make him well. He was admitted to hospital *forty-three* times. Many days he would spend in intensive care. Countless times we were told "he will not make it this time" and I kept on arguing with God.

When he was twelve-years-old, he got blood poisoning from spoiled ice cream given to him by someone else. He was very, very sick. Weighed only 32lb. This time I finally gave up. I finally believed the doctors. We stood at his bed prayed and gave him over to our Heavenly Father. I was at peace. I felt so calm inside. A quiet joy. A sure knowledge that he would be with God. The next morning, we were told he is sitting up and eating. I cannot explain the turmoil I went through. I had finally given this son to God; finally stopped fighting. It was like an unexpected birth, but also as if God had returned my gift to Him. When God took my mother, I was angry at Him. Now He did not take my son and I almost felt the same. That is also the day my resentment faded away. During those twelve long years, my God and my husband took turns carrying me and I did not even know, or understand this. To God be the praise.

For the first year of his life I never left Adrian's side. No sitter for him. I did not trust anyone and when we finally did bow to pressure, we were called home within half an hour and had to rush him to hospital.

I did NOT feel special, because I was chosen as the mother of this child. I *did not* feel extra strength, even if others told me I would receive this. At times I felt like an animal, wanting to protect him from others.

He became a healthy and strong man. Healthy in body and mind. Truly God has given us a miracle! This son is now married with 6 children. He has his own business and is very well liked in the community. I can never look at him, without feeling so thankful.

Unto the hills I lift my eyes. Psalm 121.

I wrote all this to encourage all those who have given birth to 'Miracle' babies.

Happy Little Boy's Day

They found him sitting on a rock and crying.

First stop was the store. All three of them bought swimming trunks, plastic pails, small shovels, snorkel goggles, and cheap plastic air mattresses. One of the boys bought all theirs in fluorescent green and the others in yellow and pink. Next stop was Mom's. There they made a stack of peanut butter and jam sandwiches and the largest jug of Kool-Aid that they could make. They also packed chocolate chip cookies, three boxes of raisins, a box of crackers, and three apples. My son gave me the 'do not ask questions look'.

They left at eleven o'clock in the morning to go to the beach for the day. Three young men attired and equipped as small boys. They built a sandcastle with a moat and carried endless pails of water to fill the moat. They played close to the water and also 'swam' in ankle deep water on top of their air mattress, sporting their goggles and snorkels. They walked miles along the beach gathered shells and cool stones. They decorated the castle with it. They ate all the sandwiches and bought a chocolate ice cream cone from the vendor and smeared it all over their faces. Then washed it off right in the lake. They came home sunburned, tired, dirty, and red-eyed. All three of them.

When they found him, he had told him about how he grew up. About the constant abuse at the hands of his father. About the abuse his mom and the kids suffered. He cried when he told them that he had never had a 'happy little boys day'.

His friends love him.

Now twenty-six years later, all in their forties, they are still the best of friends. Bonded forever over a 'happy little boys day'.

Our Special Needs

He runs through the park;
His blond curls dancing on his head.
He is a sunbeam;
A sunbeam of love.

His eyes are so blue;
So endless blue.
His laughter so happy.
This child. This joy. This boy.

Yes, I hear them talking.
Yes, I hear their speech.
Yes, I hear their whisper.
He is special needs.

Yes, I hear them talking.
Yes, I hear their speech.
Yes, I hear their whisper.
For they are special needs.

Father, Creator and Lord of us all:
You gave us our children.
How thankful my heart sings!
Reflecting Your love,
Reflecting Your image,
This gift from above.

This knowledge, so sure now.
My heart sings and beats.
Knowing you're with me.
In my special needs.

Reflections

There are thirteen children in the class. All of them special needs. Ten are confined to wheelchairs, three walk unaided, none of them talk and all wear diapers. This is my first time. I feel a great anxiety in the pit of my stomach.

Bobby is assigned to me. He is one of the walking ones.

The teacher tells me "He is autistic and sometimes responds to sign language."

I sign 'Hi, how are you?'. Bobby does not respond. The teacher puts Bobby's hand in mine. It feels like a dead fish. His head hangs down. I take Bobby to the small wading pool and sit him down.

"Dear Father in heaven, I do not know what to do with this child."

I pry open Bobby's hand and put a toy in it. Bobby does not respond. I sit down next to him with about a foot between us. I do not try to make him look at me and I start to talk to him softly.

Week after week I do the same thing. I talk. I tell Bobby about my grandchildren, about my children, the cost of gas at the pump the total, the mileage on our car, the society I belong to, the problems in the church, the economy, and the weather. I explain why we have our house for sale and that we plan to build a house on a lot in the country. Bobby does not respond.

The last five minutes are always spent in the hot tub. I take Bobby's hand and say, "Come to the hot tub with me."

He comes and sits on the steps, up to his waist in the water and won't move. It takes two people to push him aside so other people can enter the hot tub.

During week seven of working with Bobby, a miracle happened. Bobby looked up when he entered the pool area and let go of the teacher's hand, walked across the floor and takes my hand. I dare not say or do anything to him. Together we walk to the wading pool. I begin to talk as I always do. Bobby still does not respond. When it is time to go to the hot tub, I continue talking. I say, "Bobby if you want to go to the hot tub, you have to take me." "Take my hand, pull me up and let's go."

Bobby fills a little watering can twice more and slowly pours it out. Then Bobby responds! He gets up. He does not look at me. He takes my hand and pulls! Together we walk to the hot tub. He leads, I follow.

Bobby sits on the steps up to his waist in the water. It takes two people to move him so others can enter the pool.

The next week, Bobby again took me to the hot tub. Again he sat on the steps up to his waist in the water.

I said, "Bobby, you can sit there, but if someone comes and wants to go in the tub, you have to move."

Bobby does not respond. He just hangs his head and rocks his body.

Suddenly a voice say, "Excuse me buddy, can I get into the hot tub?"

Bobby moves and sits beside me.

I say very quietly, "Bobby you have very good manners."

Bobby sits and then very slowly he turns his head, looks at me, and *smiles*. It is the most beautiful smile I have ever seen. Bobby again hangs his head, back in his own little world. I also hang my head, for no one is to see the tears that are running down my face.

"Bless the Lord, O my soul and all that is within me, bless His Holy Name."

The Smile

We sit.
We pray.
We listen
We worship.
She turns her head
and smiles at me.

And I know,
That she knows,
That I know,
That she loves me.

For she knows
That I know,
That she knows,
That I love her.

So we sit.
We listen,
We worship,
And we pray.

Our hearts gladden within us.
We worship
with Joy.

Memory Mattress

We got ourselves one of those memory foam mattresses. First that scared me, for why would a mattress want to remember what went on in bed? We got it brand new. Still in the package for forty-five dollars. Good deal! We ripped the plastic off and out came this little funny looking thingy that was about three feet by four feet. We had been told it will take up to three days to become a big mattress. After three hours, Andy wanted to throw it out. That man has so much patience. I talked him into waiting the three days. This morning we went and looked in the motor home and the mattress now laid like a drunk across the bed; spilling over the sides and looking menacing. Sure hope it has stopped growing. Got the sheets and coverings on it and will be trying this bed out tonight. Taking four granddaughters camping soon.

Stress Free

We left for our trip on Monday morning early. At least that was the plan. Our children had told Andy to make sure the trip was without stress. I had piled all the things to take with us on the kitchen table and Andy would take it to the camper and put it on the bed. I would then in turn, put things in place. He surprised me and put all the things away. For the next three weeks, neither one knew where anything was. Stress free! We left late. The first service station had no diesel fuel, neither had the second. Before we got to the third we ran out of fuel and Andy had to go and hitch hike while I sat in the middle of an busy intersection. Stress free! We had bought the biggest bag off sunflower seeds you could get for nibbling on. They were salted and Andy had turned the fridge so high that all the fresh veggies were frozen. Stress free!

We were way, way behind schedule and so we drove and drove without stopping, whilst I drank too much water. No time for a pee break. I had to go so badly, but Andy told me we had no time to stop. He told me to go to the bathroom in the camper – to leave the door open and do not pull the bathroom out.

"It will work." he said, "Nobody looks inside a motor home to see if there is an old lady sitting on the toilet."

I had to go so badly, I thought I'd give it a try. I pulled down my pants just as Andy went around a curve. I shot forward, pants down my ankles and head butted the camper door. Good thing it was locked. Now my husband could suddenly stop after all. Well, I made it to the bathroom before he did. He had to do his own pee dance now. Even with my pants down, I was faster than him. Stress Free!

We made it across the border that first day, but could not find an RV park to sleep, so we pulled into an rest area. I refused to undress. I was sure some cop would come and tell us to move out. I unhooked my bra and crawled into bed. Andy had to go first because he does not drink water all day and does not have to get up at least three times during the night. Just then he asked me to get the flashlight from under the front seat. 'Okay,' I thought, 'I will get it'. I stepped on a plastic bag and dove to the front, landing with my right eye right smack on the stick shift. I still managed to find the flashlight. Going to sleep was easy, one eye was already closed. Stress Free!

The next morning, we woke up to snow and a freezing cold motor home. I begged Andy to take me to the nearest restaurant for *bacon, eggs, hashbrowns, toast, and coffee!*

Andy took one look at my face and said, "Yes dear."

I was so cold and we had to go outside to turn on the gas for the heating. I grabbed my coat and said, "Come, let's go let's go."

In the restaurant, I finally started to warm up again. I took my coat off and wondered why the waitress looked at me so funny. She left us and gales of laughter came from the kitchen. I looked down my chest and noticed the 'girls' footloose and fancy free resting on my top roll, while out of my right sleeve half my bra was hanging out.

Stress Free! I am sure you could not tell where my face ended and my red T-Shirt started.

Oh yes, when we returned last night we noticed three trees had fallen against the fence and the house. Not too much damage. Stress Free? What is that?

Twelve at a Time

A number of years ago, we visited my brother in Ontario. He told us that for the last five years he had been going to Cuba about three times a year to bring in Bibles and medical supplies. The people were so poor they needed *everything*. Right then and there we decided that once we were retired, we would go on a trip to Cuba with him! This past October we finally went. We had with us, twelve Bibles, two bikes, four hundred sewing needles, four hundred and twenty pens, three hundred toothbrushes, forty small toys, twenty spools of thread and lots of used clothing. We thought that we were totally prepared and were sure that my brother who was already experienced in this activity, would be able to look after us throughout the trip. But then we found out that my brother was not going to be able to come with us. We were on our own. That's when we realized that our approach had been all wrong. It was not on a man, but rather on God that we had to rely.

Going Through Customs

It is illegal to bring anything new into Cuba. Used clothing is allowed, but that is all they will allow. You can bring Bibles, but no more than twelve per couple. If you bring in more bibles, it is considered propaganda and they will simply take them and burn them. Twelve Bibles does not seem like much, but it is twelve more Bibles than they had before. When we got to customs in Cuba my husband Andy was held up. It took them fifteen minutes to compare his picture with the one in his passport. Here I stood, shaking in my boots in front of the customs clerk, who was waving our English Bible around. I just stood there and prayed. There was no way that we could hide all that stuff we took along!

He then picked up a Spanish Bible. "How about this one?" he said.

Suddenly I found inner strength, I looked him straight in the eye and said, "Everything that you see, they are gifts for our friends and your people here. There are three more suitcases and they all have the same thing in them. Gifts for your people."

"What are the names of your friends?" he asked.

"George (Jorge) and Blanca," I replied.

He waved us on and never even looked in the other suitcases. We were the last ones to be checked and everyone else was scrutinized, but us he waved on. We thanked our almighty God and walked on.

Searching for Christians

My brother, had told us how to make contact with the Christians.

"It is quite simple really." he said, "You pray quite openly for your meals and someone will approach you and ask if you are a Christian. He will then direct you to the nearest group of Christians or church."

Well, we did that, but it did not work. The Lord had other plans for us.

We could not have prayed more openly than we did. We had arrived on Friday and by Saturday no one had yet approached us. The staff at our hotel told us it was about a one-kilometer walk to town and we figured we could do that. Again we prayed that the Lord would lead us to Christians and we started walking.

This is a communist country, so first we had to walk past a guard. Nothing happened and we continued down the road. Suddenly a girl with three small children came out of the bushes.

She said, "Hi, my name is Melissa, want to come to my house?"

We had been warned that beggars would come out of the bushes, so we said, "No, but we are looking for Iglesia Protestante (Protestant Church) and also for Blanca and Jorge."

She said she didn't know about the church but she did know Blanca and agreed to take us to her. She indeed took us to Blanca's house and when we mentioned Clarence, Blanca hugged us and invited us into her home. Clarence and his wife, Marcia, had visited two years before and she still remembered them. She showed us her home. It was just two rooms about eight by ten feet each and a lean-to about five by eight. There were no windows, just openings in the cement wall. And though she had a beautiful ceramic floor there was no front door, just an old curtain.

She pulled me into her lean-to. "Look." she said. "Look I have food, much food."

I could have cried. She had about two cups of rice and two cups of brown beans, that was all.

We visited about ten homes during our stay and that was the only time we actually saw some food. People there have no closets or cabinets, so when you walk in their houses you can see all that they have.

Blanca had two children. Her lean-to held three plates, one soup bowl, three forks, two knives, one spoon, two small pans, and that was it.

There is equality in communist countries; they are all equally poor. They do all have free utilities though. Andy had to duck because the free power was hooked up; the live wires hung from the ceiling since they have no lights. All of the houses have a fridge, but except for a cola bottle full of water, Blanca's fridge was empty. All of the women have a sewing machine, but no needles or thread. They have free medical care, but they don't even have Band-Aids or Tylenol. They can write out a prescription, but cannot fill it.

Lunch

Blanca was very gracious. We gave her family toothbrushes and pens and then left. Outside, Melissa was waiting.

"Please," she said, "I now know an Iglesia (Church) in Pilon twenty kilometers away."

Blanca had said there was no church or Christians nearby so we decided to go with Melissa to her house.

Again we saw great poverty. There were about thirty people and nothing in the house to eat. Most of the children were completely naked. They possessed only two chairs and we had to sit while they looked at us. We sort of promised to come back with more gifts and only gave them a toothbrush this time. Melissa came outside with us and told us that if we were there at nine o'clock the next morning, her brother would take us to church for ten dollars. We agreed and told her we would be there.

By then, we were ready to eat the lunch we had taken with us. We took our sandwiches out of our baggies and something strange happened. All of a sudden there were people looking at our food, with a look in their eyes we had never seen before. The look was hunger.

Wordlessly I handed my food to the nearest person and turned to Andy to ask him to do the same. He was already doing it. The woman took my sandwich and broke off a small piece and then handed it to the next person. There was somehow a great dignity in what they were doing. No one spoke. They all just ate.

Visiting a Brothel

Back at the hotel, we were told Melissa was a prostitute and to stay away from her. Now what were we going to do? Again we turned to God in prayer and Sunday morning found us waiting for Melissa, outside the compound away from the guards. We didn't let the guards see the car we left in. It was a 1955 Lada. We had to go twenty kilometers to the town of Pilon. It was about thirty-five degrees outside the car, never mind the inside temperature. The car broke down four times on the way up and four more times on the way back. "No problem, we fix," our drivers would say and on the side of the so-called road they would monkey around and fix it. We were also treated to some very loud rock music throughout the trip. I, for one, will never forget that trip.

For five hundred feet at a time we would drive in the ditch, because the ditch was in better shape than the road.

All through the drive Melissa kept eyeing our backpacks and offering to hold them. Finally I opened one backpack and gave her a Bible. I know she hoped for a blouse, but she thanked me anyway.

When we arrived at the church we found it had a front door but the side was totally open. During the service, pigs and goats wandered in freely and were promptly chased out. We were welcomed, given a Gideon Bible and seated in the front of the church where a young man, Merardo, offered to translate the sermon for us as it was being preached.

The people knew what Melissa did for a living and a snicker ran through the church. We gave all of our Bibles to the pastor and after checking each one, he handed them out. There were about ten Bibles for the one hundred and fifty people. Never have we seen such rejoicing, upon receiving the word of God, as we witnessed that day. They were even more excited because it was the whole Bible, the New Testament too!

The sermon was on a portion of Genesis, about Abraham, Hagar and Sara and the fact that Abraham had a son with Hagar. This was an act of unbelief and disobedience, the minister said. He then warned the congregation against people like Melissa. Problems in their families were caused by the unfaithfulness of the men, he said, and that had to stop because the Lord forbade it.

The previous night Andy and I had made up our minds to use Melissa as a guide to go to church but that we would not go with her anywhere else, or give her anything else. Now Melissa sat next to me in church. She was reading the passage and kept looking things up in her Bible. Slowly a tear slid down her face and for the rest of the sermon she quietly cried and our hearts melted. She introduced us to her nephew and niece and we promised them we would bring something for them to Melissa's house.

The following Monday we set off to visit Melissa. We had with us shirts, pens, toy's, and more. We certainly did not feel comfortable at her house, now that we knew what the girls did for a living. A brothel is simply not a good place to be. We handed out our gifts and left as fast as we could. We also gave Melissa gifts for her niece and nephew and stressed to the other girls that these gifts weren't for them but were for Melissa to take to her relatives.

After that ordeal was over we walked to Blanca's house with our gifts for her and her family. While we were there, a girl from the brothel came and told us to come because the people in the brothel were being real mean to Melissa. We said sorry, but we weren't going to go there again.

Later on, we rented mopeds and again went to Pilon. A lady at our hotel had given us money for the church but did not dare go there herself. When we got to the outskirts of Pilon, there walking along the road, was Melissa! She had been kicked out of the house of ill repute and everything except her Bible had been taken from her. She was going home to her parents. She asked us to come with her, and we did. She was welcomed home with open arms and when we left, she asked, "Are you coming to Cuba again?"

"Yes," we answered.

Then she said, "Next time you come, you will not find me in the bad house, you will find me in the church."

It is something totally awesome when you realize that the Lord, who certainly did not need us, used us.

The Lord willing, we will go again next September; our goal is to bring a Bible for every family in that church.

Pastor Michael

With Pastor Michael, we become painfully aware of his lack of knowledge. He is happy with the study books we bring him. Most of them donated. One book catches his attention. We open it for him to Lord's Day 1.

He reads it and exclaims:" That is what I believe."

He has been greatly influenced by the prosperity gospel. Now he too was demanding that God come down and heal people. Demanding that the Holy Spirit come down and join his group. He screamed and yelled at the top of his lungs. We are so aware of the big language barrier. When we first attended this Church, our friend would translate for us as the minister would preach. We heard good Biblical sermons. This is no longer the case. They are all waiting for the signs and wonders to begin. He does teach the newcomers from the Bible in a separate class, but the other members are no longer being fed. One lady told us that only the ladies of the society bring the truth of the Gospel now. We can only hope and pray for God to open Pastor Michael's eyes and work in his heart.

Pastor Michael is such a likable guy. His income is very low. It is a tradition to butcher a pig on New Year's Eve. All he could offer his family was three boiled eggs. He hoped the New Year would be much better, but there were so many shortages at the market. You need a ration book and money in order to buy food. Sometimes you can buy something at the black market. There are essential illegal things you need to do in order to feed your family.

The Friday before we came, his family simply had nothing to eat and he apologized for not inviting us for a meal. The Cuban people had run out of beans and now there was no rice available at the market. The sad part is, that by giving them money, they still cannot buy at the market, for they have no ration coupons. Yes, there is the black market, but do not think that they have plenty for sale. No beans, nor rice available. Some of the stronger men did manage to get the little rice that was available, but Pastor Michael explained that as a pastor, he could not join in the fights at the markets.

He has a wife and three children. He was happy with the Bibles, study books, clothing and shoes he received for his family. Happy with the notebooks and pens for his students. Yet I was choking back tears, because we could not bring him food.

The Shoes

We had again arrived in Cuba. Arrival was on a Wednesday. We spent all day Thursday finding a car to rent. Finally, at four pm, we got a car. All of us hot and tired. Suddenly I felt I had to do something. I ran to the room, frantically searching through all the suitcases for running shoes. I found four pairs. Various sizes and by miracle, all as good as new. I pleaded with Andy to drive us to Pilon.

"Now?" he said.

"Yes now."

Andy did not feel like it, but I felt such an urgency. It simply had to be done tonight.

"I know, I know, we will go there tomorrow, but we need to go and bring those shoes tonight." I did not know, nor could I understand, why I felt we could not wait until the next day. I remember almost crying, while pleading with him to take me.

Andy gave in, tired as he was, for nothing is more tiring then waiting all day for a car to rent.

It is only a twenty minute drive. The family I wanted to go and see did not know we were in Cuba again. We drove to Pilon and found their house. Happiness flooded my soul as we called out to them. "We are here, can we come in?"

We hugged and I opened the bag with the four pairs of running shoes and asked her husband and three sons to please try them on. Suddenly silence and then tears. Yes, the shoes fit. All four of them fit as if they were meant for them and they *were* meant for them.

Tears flowed as the mom tried to explain; crying and praising God at the same time. Tears, because just the night before, the family had met in prayer to ask God for a pair of running shoes for the middle boy. Without shoes, he was not allowed in school and if the parents did not send him to school, they would be fined. So they prayed and asked for one pair of used shoes. God heard them and gave fourfold. We laughed, cried and prayed together. A grateful thanksgiving prayer to our Lord and Master.

It is an awesome feeling to have felt and seen the Hand of God firsthand.

Two Ways to Live

Yes, we had started to study this book. Only took two sessions before our trip to Cuba. I took the book with me and kept thinking about it as I looked at the way some Cuban people lived. Or maybe I should say 'had to live'. Because I had brought my daughter, daughter-in-law and four granddaughters, I looked with different eyes this time.

I looked at the tourists. Tourists means 'people going around in circles'. Our friends and Andy and I had been travelers. Travelers mean 'being in travail with the people'. Quite a few were indeed travelers, helping Cuban people. Many had been there forty, fifty, or even more than one hundred times. But there were also quite a few older and younger men who were just looking for a young Cuban girl. They pay for a girl to join them for a week at the hotel and are quite openly bragging about this. Sick perverts. The hotel has a policy. No one under eighteen is allowed and the age difference must not exceed twenty-five years. It is no problem finding willing girls, for it means income for her and help for their extended family. Incredibly sad.

I also saw a fair amount of lonely widows and single, middle-aged girls. They too seemed to have come for the same reason as the men. Just as sad. The same policies also apply to them. Marriage to a Canadian and possibly moving to Canada is the dream of many. Oh yes, some have found true love; some have found a lasting relationship. I do not discount this at all.

Because of a young girl and young man who both sang so very beautiful, we came to know the entertainers. Almost every night they came and joined the entertainers, to sing for the tourists. They hoped that this way, a door would open to a rewarding future in the music world. Both of them were married and each had a young child. We talked to them almost every time when they came to sing. They did not get paid for this and arrived hungry. We started slipping them food and gave presents for their babies. By the second week, they were told not to accept food from tourists, so they also now left hungry. The young girl eagerly accepted a Bible from one of the granddaughters. The young man declined.

We visited the girl's home. Two rooms: both about eight by ten feet. They shared a bathroom with the neighbors. The young woman was so sweet! She was so happy and proud to show us her home. Happy she could offer us her strong sweet coffee.

The young man asked us to come and also visit his home. He wanted us to meet his wife and ten-month-old child. I promised him a visit during the next trip and two weeks later we did. We learned that his parents had been members of the Church, but no longer came. Also his wife had at one time come to Church. He came to us and asked us for a Bible. Thankfully we still had some. We visited his house. An eight by ten foot room, added to his in-law's house. That was all they had.

One of the other entertainers was also present in this house. He told us he had two daughters living in Havana with his wife. Told us that all the entertainers had wives and children all over the place. No one was serious about their marriages. All of them had girlfriends and children with several women. As an entertainer, you go where you must go, to earn some dollars. And it was so worth it because you earn more as entertainer. At least three or four times as much.

Finally, the last day came. The last chance to talk. The last chance to witness. The last chance to tell them that there are two ways to live. I asked them if they loved their spouses. If they loved their babies and if they wanted a stable life for them. I asked them what kind of wife or husband they wanted to be. What kind of parent they wanted for their little girls. A life like the other entertainers? Just because they would have more money and food? I told them I knew that both of them had come from a Christian home. That both knew better. That both knew you could be a Christian and still sing and make music. I explained that they indeed had a choice. A choice to serve God and family or a choice to become an entertainer for the hotels and forget about their families.

I hugged them and said goodbye.

Yes, I am still praying for them. For their families. For stability.

I loved those kids.

Patty

For five weeks I have watched her. A young girl, who *did not* want to be there. Angry, very angry. That is how I would describe her. Her sister and mom came and she tagged along. Once or twice she would join the group, but most of the time she would hang back. I made a point of making contact. I noticed she seemed to look for me and wait for me to say something to her. I would of course get the usual grunt. This time was different.

We had moved the women's group to a Church building around the corner from the shelter. The mothers loved it. It was clean and they could let the kids play in the playroom. There was even a nursery for the sleeping babies. The mother and the two daughters showed up. Lisa had had her baby. She was all aglow. Patty wore an ever bigger scowl that usual. We all sat around the table, admired the new baby, called Lisa a good mom and showered her with gifts for the baby. Patty sat way back in the room.

Carrying a coffee, I moved in her direction, aware of her eyes following me. This time I asked her if she had found a job yet.

"A job?! A Job?! Mom come here!" she demanded.

Her mom walked over.

Patty said, "I want to talk to this lady and I want you to be there and I want it to be in private."

We moved way back to the back of the room. I pushed three easy chairs in a circle and said, "Ok talk."

Patty swallowed, then started telling me about her life and how she grew up. 'Mom' was her foster mom. A woman to whose house she had run to when she escaped the home she was born in. When she lived with her birth mom, she had gone to school until grade four. After that, she was kept in the basement on a foam pad. She was kept there to be used by the boyfriends her mom took home. She was given only food and drink. No clothing. She simply just *existed* for years and years. At age fifteen, she escaped and ran away to this woman's house. Her now foster mom. They had her stay overnight. This wild unkempt girl. But they took her home the next day. They thought there was something mentally wrong with her.

A week later, she again came to their house and begged them to keep her; begged them to be her mom and dad. They did keep her. The mom is helping her with reading and math. They never called the authorities. This simple couple simply just kept her. No police have ever been involved. Nothing. No financial benefit ever. They probably would not even have qualified to take her in.

Patty told me her 'sister' Lisa was mad at her because Patty just could not hold or touch the baby. She was too scared to hold it. Was afraid of dropping it. She did not know what to do with kids.

All I said to her was, "You look to me like someone who would be very good with kids."

I was to start the Bible study with the group that day. It would be the first time. Lisa and her mom left, but Patty wanted to stay.

As the ladies were gathering around the table, one of them fished her ten day old out of the stroller with one hand while trying to get a diaper out of her diaper bag with the other. Patty was just walking by to get to the table for the study. The woman stopped her and handed Patty her baby saying, "Here, hold my kid while I do this."

Patty was frozen in place. With frantic eyes she looked my way and almost ran to the chair next to me. I tried not to look her way but rather just put some books on the table and dug for pencils. The baby had its little head against her breast. Slowly Patty relaxed. She carefully touched the baby's hair. She simply looked at the baby and smiled. The mom came over and took the baby from Patty to nurse it.

We started the study. Patty read along and took notes. Big printed letters. When the baby's mom was done nursing, Patty stood up and asked her if she could hold the baby again. She rocked and stroked the baby. This was so huge. I felt I was sitting on eggshells. Here I was sitting and explaining scripture to eight ladies and praying for the girl next to me at the same time.

We spoke about all the bad things in life that can happen to a person and compared this to the life of Job. Some spoke about their struggles. They opened up. They said that sometimes God did not seem to listen. They prayed, but the door seemed closed to them. I agreed. Yes, God does close doors and He does not always answer us in a way we expect. And sometimes we stand there and only look at that closed door; fixing our eyes only on that closed door, with our backs to the big, wide windows that God had opened for us but we refused to turn around and even look. Looking at that closed door never helps. Where we go from now on, is what truly matters.

We had an excellent discussion. Patty just rocked the baby.

She hung around while we cleaned up. Every time I looked her way, she smiled at me. It took my breath away as I saw how beautiful her smile was. How beautiful her eyes were. Suddenly, without warning, she walked up to me and hugged me. She whispered in my ear, "I am looking out of the window." She then ran down the steps and disappeared.

The Kid

Half of his head is shaven. The middle part is green and the right side is bright orange. He is clean, very clean. His red jeans are ripped, showing his boxer shorts. His torn T-shirt is white and clean. He has lots of piercings and huge earlobe holes, like some African tribesman. I have not seen that since 1954.

He is talking to an old, crying, Native man. I see him go to the coffee counter and return with a coffee and a bun which he gives to the Native man. That was the last I saw of him that day.

Two weeks later, he wandered into the kitchen while Sue and I were trying to figure out how to feed about eighty people on only thirty eggs and seventy-two buns. We first decided the staff would not eat that day. No worries there as this allowed me to stick to my diet plan. Someone brought in a hot apple strudel that was six inches by twelve. We looked at it and just laughed.

He stood in the doorway as we boiled the eggs. They were very small eggs that were not good enough for sale and so were donated to the shelter. He got in my way as I was peeling the eggs. Suddenly he found himself with a spoon and knife in his hand.

"Cut the eggs right through the middle and scoop out the egg then dump it in the green bowl." The old lady, me, had spoken.

He looked at me funny but then went to work. One of the other guys ran out and got a jar of Mayo. In no time at all, we had egg salad on the buns and got the kid to bring out the trays to the hungry.

When all the buns were gone and the apple strudel was still on the counter, the kid got busy. He ran to the back freezer and came back with ice cream. Two half full pails: one chocolate and one strawberry. It was just the two of us in the kitchen. He found the styrofoam soup bowls and plastic spoons. We divided the strudel into some sixty pieces and added the two kinds of ice cream. When he carried the first tray out, he was greeted with a shout of *"Dessert!"*

Sue came back and took the second tray. He came back into the kitchen and again it was just the two of us working together. When everything was gone, he suddenly said, "The way I live, I have about ten to fifteen years to live."

"So do I," I informed him dryly.

He glanced up at me with a stunned look on his face.

"I had fun," he said. "Got drunk every day. That's why I am here. Community service. Can't wait to get back to drinking."

"First time?" I asked him.

"No, the second and the last time," he said.

I agreed and told him that the third time would probably be jail and even more fun.

He asked, "Well did you have a fun life?"

"Sure did and with no splitting headache in the morning! Besides that, I can even remember the fun I had." I asked him if he'd ever played in a band, toured Europe by motorbike or traveled all over the world. I told him that I completely understood that going to a bar and spending the evening drinking and then staggering around with a splitting headache was, of course much more fun. But at least I had fun for more years than he had had.

We cleaned the kitchen, no longer talking. Before he left, he told me he had six more hours to serve and probably would not see me again. I agreed with him and told him I realized that it would be jail for him.

He left but came back a little while later. "Look," he said, "if I ever want to be told off, can I look you up?"

"Sure, be glad to," I replied. We grinned and shook hands!

So now there is another kid in my prayers and I do not even know his name.

Willing Partner

(Fiction)

I am walking down the hallway, talking and laughing with my friends. This dame is going to talk about sexual abuse and I so don't want to go. I so don't want to listen. I do *not* want to sit in the back, because they will expect the victims to sit there and I am *not* a victim. But I also do not want to sit in the first row, so I move along, still laughing and talking whilst aiming for the middle seats.

Not a bad looking dame. I have no intention on concentrating on what she has to say. She said she was a victim, Yeah right. Probably some guy made a pass at her in high school and now she is a victim. Cry me a river lady. She talks. I don't want to hear and I don't want to listen. My tongue finds the sharp edge on one of my molars. By pushing my tongue against the tooth I can keep a straight face. I will not show emotion. I will not show emotion. Grandpa has told me, I am *not* a victim. I am a willing partner and no one would believe me anyway. I clean his house every Saturday and I bike down to his place to do it. That means I am a willing partner.

She charged him? She did? They believed her? Oh of course not. They found him not guilty, so why bother. Grandpa said I do not have to come on Saturday. He will just phone my mom and ask for my sister to come. I wish I was dead. I am dead inside and so alone. I wish he was dead. Why can't he have a heart attack and die, like other grandpas do. Why do I have to have a healthy grandpa? Oh? Others came forward? There were more? And he was found guilty? Great! Probation, is that all? See what's the use of coming forward. Not believed. No jail. Nothing except now everyone knows your secret.

She seems like a great lady and a fighter.

But for me, I am a willing partner.

The Good Shepherd

"The good shepherd lays down his life
for the sheep." (John 10:11)
".. and they shall be whiter than snow." (Psalm 51:7)

His sheep stand around. They talk and they bleat.

The Shepherd steps down and goes in search of the lost.

He leaves His flock to search for His loved ones,
for find them He will, He knows where to seek.

In the bars and the shelters, the malls of the earth.
The hotels, the motels, the dumpsters and the
crawlspaces. The downtrodden and meek.

For those who live by faith and walk on water, go
surefooted to the land. But those who cry for love
and compassion, to those He reaches His hand.

The Shepherd, He finds them and carries them
home. He washes them cleaner and whiter than
snow. The angels rejoice, the world is aglow.

But the sheep stand around in their not too clean coats.
Yes, the sheep stand around and they bleat.
Yes, they bleat!

Depression

August 12th, 2014

The little violin player.
We loved him, oh so much.
He smiled and winked at all of us.
He was so handsome, so cute!

And in his heart a pain so deep.
A pain that kept him from his sleep.
A pain that fed on him as host.
Enfolded in darkness, he was so lost.

So gifted, so talented, so brilliant.
She did her parents proud.
A future bright and without care,
They all would seek her out.

And in her heart a pain so deep.
A pain that kept her from her sleep.
A pain that fed on her as host.
Enfolded in darkness, she was so lost.

A self-made man. Successful, yes.
He had it all. Respect, and no wants.
Smart kids, great wife.
A home in the best neighborhood.

And in his heart a pain so deep.
A pain that kept him from his sleep.
A pain that fed on him as host.
Enfolded in darkness, he was so lost.

Her home was clean, her children good.
Her friends admired this super-mom.
Always helping, always ready.
Serving her husband, neighbors and friends.

And in her heart a pain so deep.
A pain that kept her from her sleep.
A pain that fed on her as host.
Enfolded in darkness, she was so lost.

A darkness so deep, so without hope.
A darkness they could not explain.
A darkness so deep, they just can't get out.
A darkness, so hopeless. Such pain.

It is not, that they did not want to live.
It is not, that they did not love.
It is not, lack of care for those left behind.
It was simply a yearning for God.

A wanting to go to their Heavenly mansion.
To a place prepared just for them.
To a place without darkness.
To a place without pain.
Yes, pain.

That heavy, heavy, dark, black, weight.
Invisible to all.
That weight, oh Jesus, lift for us.
And grant us joy.
Not pain.

Pain

There is a pain that no one knows.
There is a pain that never shows.
It lies so deep within my soul.
It is a joy that someone stole.
How come that after many years,
it still rekindles all the fears
that dominated my married life
and overshadowed me as wife?
Why did I have to lose my mother?
To me she was like no one other.
I so badly wanted to see,
my children laughing on her knee.
I find no ease.

The gifts of God that I have received.
My children and I so believed,
that with God's help I would someway
teach them to live, to love and pray.
To walk in faith and be so blessed
and never had I even guessed,
that one would leave and go to God.
I am not ready, no I'm not.
I am so lonely, so alone.
My sins for which I can't atone,
My God I cry to you alone.
I find no peace.

Psalm 84: Sunday June 23rd, 2014

We sing and my mind wanders.
We sing and I am not prepared.
My heart and flesh is numb today
and fails to honor God.

The swallow swiftly builds a nest.
Oh no, I cannot sing.
For yes, He would look after them.
I so do feel the sting.

I choke and oh I try to sing.
The words are without joy.
My mask is slipping quickly now
and then, I see the boy.

His face lights up, he nudges Dad.
See what we're going to sing?
I know this song. I know it loud!
The joy shines from his eyes.

He lifts his face towards his Dad.
So Dad can truly see,
that yes he does know every word.
This song, that speaks to me.

From strength to strength, before thy face.
Dear God help also me.
Teach me again to clearly see.
This God of Grace.

Grant me oh God, this simple joy,
of knowing all your songs.
Thank You, for sending me this boy.
And give me peace,
Oh Lord.

Consider the Lilies of the Field

As my head pushes out of the deep,
out of the dust of the earth.
As sunlight embraces me
with delight.
Then slowly.
Very slowly.
A leaf unfurls;
one after another.
The morning rejoices.
The petals spread,
lapping up the sun.
Until I stand proud and straight.
Rejoicing in the goodness and greatness of God.

Then,
Carelessly.
Unwittingly.
Unknowingly.
A speck, just a speck of dirt,
is kicked on a glorious petal.
And I curl this petal.
Tight.
Very tight.
And slowly.
Very slowly.
I roll up, leaf after leaf.
Shrinking.

Withdrawing.
And pulling myself
back into the safety
of the deep dark earth
where I *remain*
in a fetal position.

Ask, Seek, Knock

"Ask and it will be given to you, seek and
you will find; knock and the door will
be opened to you." (Matthew 7:7)

ASK!
Lord, why should I ask you?
Don't I know it all?
I talk the talk and walk the walk.
And yet on You I call.

SEEK!
I seek You all the day Lord
and yet I do not find.
I talk the talk and walk the walk.
It hurts my heart and mind.

KNOCK!
I know the door is open
and yet, I stand and knock.
I talk the talk and walk the walk.
Alone amongst the flock.

When oh when, will I truly understand,
Your love and understanding of my unasked questions.
When will I truly understand, that you found me?

And truly see
and understand
the need to knock.
For I belong,
To
YOU!

Timor, Indonesia

Iman

He just sat there. Looking scared and intimidated. Skinny arms folded across his torn shirt. Big brown eyes looking at the lady. Trying to take it all in. Nodding his head solemnly, while making all those promises.

Yes, he would study hard.

Yes, he would obey his teachers.

Yes, he would faithfully attend school.

School? Did his heart dare to hope? Did he truly have a sponsor? A sponsor who would send him to school, buy him shoes, schoolbag, supplies and a uniform?

Iman's heart was bursting. Did he show his joy, his happiness? No, he just continued looking solemnly at the lady. He did not show his happiness at all. But when we saw him leave the house, he suddenly took a little skip and then another one. Then he started jumping up and down and calling out to his friends, "I have a sponsor! I have a sponsor!"

Their thirst for education. Their hunger to learn. You can almost taste it. You can see it in the eyes of the children. They are so aware. Education is their ticket out of the hunger and despair. They prayed for so many years. The possibility of a school and learning to write and read always seemed out of reach, but now, there is indeed hope.

The trade school had just opened. Young men lined up around the block. There was maybe room for forty-five young men to learn a trade. A trade, so they could make a living. If one person in the family has a job, everyone in the family eats. They took in one hundred students that day. One hundred received the gift of a future.

The young man who had waited in line as number 101, committed suicide that day. May God have mercy.

Selfi and Seni

There were two girls from the Island of Savu. One was seventeen and the other eighteen years old. The older one had a non-Christian boyfriend. Both the girls have a grade three education. Their father came for help. Could we help somehow to make the girls more independent. We offered a sewing course. That had worked for two other girls who now make all the uniforms for the school. No the girls did not want to take a sewing course. They wanted to farm. They wanted a goat farm. This means you get a goat and when it has a kid you can milk it and sell the milk. You walk all day with the goats and find grass to eat for them along the roads and rivers. A group of ladies, sponsored the girls and paid for one goat each, cost per goat was forty-five dollars. The girls did well and the society wanted to buy them another goat. With two goats the girls would be independent and not need to marry this boy. This non-Christian boy.

Selfi and Seni were happy with the goats. Selfi, the one with the boyfriend, wanted to break up with him. The boyfriend was also a very controlling and abusive person. Her parents did not know that she was afraid of him and afraid to break up with him. He had told her, "If you break up with me I will kill you and your family." She was so scared to tell her parents, until one day she could not take it anymore and told him it was over. That day was also the day that her father had gone to the sponsor office to get the money for the second set of goats. It is an eight and a half hour trek to the office. That night the boyfriend set fire to the house. He also had a knife with him. They screamed for help and the neighbors heard them and came to help. The neighbors caught him. The father was so angry that he took the guy to the police in Kupang. The same eight and a half hours again. When you have someone arrested in Timor, you pay for his keep and the court fees and any other expenses. This is the way things are done in Indonesia. Of course he was full of remorse when he came to tell the folks at the office what he had done with the goat money. He offered to sell some of his land to pay for the goats.

We had a dilemma. If the farmer sells a piece of property, he will be able to pay for the goats himself, but his income will go down and he will produce less rice for his wife and eleven children. Yet, if we do not ask for the money back, they might think that the office has an endless supply and others might find reasons to use sponsor money for other uses. Besides that, there would always be the blame and shame on the girl. We told him to keep his land and that he has to pay back the ninety dollars, but he can do it over a long period; one dollar or fifty cents a month. We also showed him that the Bible said that no interest should be charged.

He and his family are happy they saved face and did not blame and shame. The ex-boyfriend is behind bars.

Isak and Rani

When we visited Isak's home to bring a letter from his sponsor, we found a seven pound baby. There is nothing unusual in finding a seven pound baby, but this one was only one year old. The mother had no milk and you do not grow from rice water. To buy formula would cost twenty-four dollars per year. Twenty-four dollars to save a life.

And then there was Rani. His family had heard about the new Christian Junior High School. Rani wanted to go there. It is a five and a half hour trek to go to the new school, but when the new school opened, Rani was there. He had no schoolbag, no shoes, and no uniform. He also had no sponsor, but Rani did not know that. He trusted that he would be looked after and he was. He was not the only one that showed up without being registered. Seven more showed up, all from the Island of Rote. All without sponsors.

The office emailed me and asked what should they do. I told them to buy the children shoes, books, uniforms, and supplies.

"Good," they said, as they had already done so.

That week again I learned of the providence of God. Every day the mail brought me checks. Little checks, a birthday party gift, instead of more presents, checks without explanations; just made out to our organization.

At the end of the week when I sent the funding to Timor we included the five hundred and ten dollars that had come from nowhere.

The office asked, "How did you know we spent five hundred and two dollars?"

I explained that we did not know, but the Lord knew. This is how we got a slush fund of eight dollars.

Truly, the Lord provides.

Opa

In 1999, the small churches in Timor were overrun by refugees. East Timor had declared its independence and refugees came across the border. The Church in the little village did what it could. They fed, clothed and sheltered them. To put it simply, they, the refugees, were not nice people.

When they finally were settled into refugee camps, a special needs girl in the Church, was found to be pregnant. In May of 2000, Opa was born. His mother is not able to look after him. She and Opa live with her mother. She is a seventy year old widow. The grandmother supports herself, her daughter and Opa with a vegetable garden. She plants them and waters them by hand, every single day. Then she takes the vegetables to market to sell. Before grandma goes to work, she feeds and changes Opa. She then puts him to bed again, until she returns. Do you know that after a while, a child like that does not cry anymore? He does not get stimulated, not played with, not read to. No stories are told to him. Nobody teaches him how to clap his hands. A child like that does not even grow. His mother is not able to do it and his grandmother is too busy providing food for him.

Opa is the first student to enter kindergarten at two and a half years old. He now has a whole bunch of brothers and sisters. They love him to pieces and Opa thrives! They taught him how to walk and talk. Even potty trained him! They loved him and made him one of them. They became his family.

God is good. So good.

Emergency Landing

Today is the first day of the rest of our life.

We left this morning for Sabu Island. A small propeller plane with about twelve passengers aboard. I sat right up front behind the pilot. It was very interesting. On the other side, also up front, was a man with one arm. He had had it amputated just this week. In front of him in a carton box was his arm. He would not leave his arm in the hospital. No, he had to take it back to his island. The arm was packed in a plastic bag with formaldehyde. I noticed the carton box was getting wet and a strange smell started filling the plane. That is when we discovered it was formaldehyde. No mask or anything in the plane for us to use. They moved the box away from the front near the pilot, to the back and radioed for help. A box of tissues was passed around for the passengers. I had a hankie and covered my nose and mouth with it.

I felt very calm and turned around to look at my husband. We just smiled at each other. I thought back to our first emergency plane landing. That was way back on our honeymoon. Then too, I had felt this calmness. This sure knowledge of being in God's hands. If this was the end, it was fine with us. No panic, just trust. It is awesome to experience the absence of fear.

The pilot was ordered to fly back. Everyone started having problems breathing and my eyes started stinging. The pilot was in a bad way but we made it back and that is what counted. The pilot passed out just as we landed. All the doors opened and we could breathe again. Praise God from who all blessings flow.

We could not fly again that day. The flight was rescheduled for the next day. Our friend, a local doctor, had seen the plane return. He came right over and checked us out. Our host and I, were sent to bed and we slept for eight hours straight. Andy, being six-foot-four, did not inhale as much of the formaldehyde and was perfectly ok. Other than a little dizzy, we were perfectly alright.

Yes, in His hands.

Carlo and Ronald

Carlo. Carlo's mom is deadly ill. All their funds have gone to the doctor. The family owes ten million RP to the doctor. about fifteen hundred dollars. Yesterday, his dad died suddenly due to an asthma attack.

Carlo is sixteen. His brother lives in east Timor and his sister in Florence. He has to shoulder all the responsibility. The body has to be transported for burial. The neighbors are raising funds. Carlo is a student in Grade eleven. His classmates and Wendy went to see him.

Wendy came back crying. "So very poor." she said.

Carlo had broken down when he saw his friends. They are not sure if he will return to school. He is the provider now. His friends went out and collected funds to help him with the funeral costs. The three of us wanted to pay for the funeral costs. The pastor told us not to.

He said, "Never take away from his friends and family, the opportunity to help."

We were allowed to donate, but not more than what would be expected of friends. We were so humbled by this experience.

Ronald. He is eighteen. Two years ago, his mother died. His dad fell out of a tree and died too. Ronald suddenly had all the responsibility. The friends cried together yesterday. Ronald lives with his brother. He works for them to pay for his keep. He gets up at three o'clock in the morning to go fishing and then sells the fish at the early market. This pays for his school fee and uniforms. By seven o'clock, he is at school. He studies hard and is the brightest student in my class. School is out at two in the afternoon. He works for his brother till six in the evening every day.

He is not a Church member, but wanted a Christian education. A girl from Canada had given him a Bible two years ago. He reads it daily, which explains his 'Bible language English'.

He will make it. He has drive and determination.

May God be with both boys. If we would help these boys, we would have fifty more lining up for help by this evening. The board warned us. They make the rules here. They will however, receive some 'undercover' help.

Ruben: Our Son

They sat on the ground, the three of them. Welian, his mom and Ruben. They sat in front of the hut they called home. That's where we came to visit them. We had first met them, or I should say heard about them, in January of 2000. It now was May 2003.

When we had first started our plan of sponsoring needy Christian children in Indonesia back in 2000, we had made strict rules. Only one child per family would at first be offered the opportunity to go to school.

Cornelius and Bertha Bunga had asked for their son Welian to be accepted and be able to go to school. But they had asked for more. Ruben Lele was a seven-year-old boy, an orphan, that Cornelius Bunga had found wandering the streets, and had taken in. Could we also help Ruben please? Cornelius had known Ruben's father and wanted to do this for his friend. We said yes. A school in Ontario sponsored both children and they both did well in school.

Twice Orphaned

Our 2003 visit came two weeks after Cornelius Bunga had died of a sudden heart attack. Sadness and grief was etched on the face of his widow. We asked her if she had made plans. What would she do now?

She looked at us. The words came out slowly. "I just don't know. I have food for two more weeks. I have no education and no skills, I only know how to be a mom and wife. Ruben will have to go!"

Incredible sadness crept over Ruben's face. At seven he had lost his parents and now at age ten will again lose his parents.

He got up, nodded at Welian and his mom and slowly walked away. His shoulders were hunched, his back so skinny and his hair already slightly reddish, showing the signs of malnutrition. He made his way down the street. Gone was his home, his family, his secure place. He had lost his opportunity to attend school. His small world had just crashed in.

We Can Help

My husband Andy looked at me and said, "Can we do something?"

We couldn't speak the language so we pleaded with our guide. "Please tell the mother we will adopt Ruben and pay her room and board to raise him for us. Please say it real loud, so Ruben can hear this."

Our guide spoke out loudly and clearly while we just watched Ruben. Ruben stopped in his tracks. We could 'see' his skinny back listening to every word.

Our guide negotiated with the mother. We had told him it should be enough to feed a family of four and Ruben listened. Slowly he turned around and came walking back. The guide was still talking, but Ruben came and again sat on the ground, right next to his mom. Slowly, ever so slowly, he turned his skinny face to us. He looked at us and us at him. A smile crept over his face. My eyes got wet. I could no longer see clearly but I know it was the most beautiful smile I have ever seen.

Ruben, the unwanted boy, was now the most wanted boy in Timor.

Praise God from whom all Blessings flow.

Reunited. You all know about Ruben, our 'adopted' son. We finally got to see them last night. We made the trip to his village. On the way over we caught some fish and cooked them at the beach to eat. So happy to see him again. He had grown and looked healthy. His eyes were bright and happy. No longer was he the shy, sick looking, little boy. His mom was beaming. Her other son. Welian. had also grown. This was one of those 'feel good about yourself and what you are doing' times.

But then, her oldest daughter showed up; skinny and carrying a sick looking little boy. We had met her four years ago. At that time, she had a two year old and was pregnant. Now again, she had a two-year-old with her. We asked about the other kids. Both of them had died due to malnutrition and infection. Gone was the good feeling. Will it ever stop? I find it so hard to see people with real hunger, real needs. People who do not say "I am starving!" No people who are starving. Her boy could not walk. He had skinny bent little legs, a protruding stomach and reddish hair. "Ricketts" she said.

Yonson tried to talk to her about drinking milk and eating fruits and vegetables. She simply said, "He does not like that kind of food, but he eats lots of plain rice three times a day."

Lack of knowledge is what is killing them. She will start coming to the office again. She will get what she needs for her boy, but does not believe it will help. The other kids had the same sickness. We both cried, but for different reasons.

Dear God, help us to truly help them.

52 Years!

January 13th, 2014

52 years ago. No, I am not going to say I married my best friend, for he was not yet my best friend. I dated him because he spoke highly of his previous girlfriends. I agreed to marry him because he prayed with me. I knew we would be one for the other and together for Christ.

We hoped, we planned, and we prayed together. Me, the city girl and him, the farm boy.

I took him to Chinese restaurants and to live shows and musicals. He took me for long drives in the country and taught me the names of trees, flowers, birds and whatever lived or grew in the country site. I liked hockey, jazz and motorbikes. He liked organ music, walking along the beach on Lake Erie and good books. I also loved reading and so we finally found something in common.

God blessed us and tested us and we often fell short. Our children were so welcomed and so loved. He worked so hard for them and had so hoped and prayed to take over his dad's farm. But it was not to be.

He loved working outside; loved working with dirt and flowers. He would always grow veggies and plants and always, he would give away what we did not need ourselves.

Our children had many health struggles, but they pulled through by God's Grace.

We tried to build memories on a very limited budget. We had fun. We also had fights. We laughed, we loved, and we cried together. We had many downs and just as many ups.

There were many times that I wanted to leave the congregation we belonged too but Andy kept me from doing so. Many times, he wanted to leave the congregation we belonged too, and then I stopped him from doing so. Truly God directed our path in those times as well, for God is faithful.

"Trust in the LORD with all your heart, and do not lean on your own understanding. In all your ways acknowledge Him, and He will make your paths straight." (Proverbs 3:5-6)

We wanted our wedding text to be Genesis 12:1-3:

"The LORD had said to Abram, "Go from your country, your people and your father's household to the land I will show you.

I will make you into a great nation, and I will bless you; I will make your name great, and you will be a blessing.
I will bless those who bless you, and whoever curses you I will curse;
and all peoples on earth will be blessed through you."

But in those days you did not ask the pastor to use a text. To this day, we do not know what text he used. So, we adopted Psalm 23.

We planned and God always had other plans and His plans were better, always. He has blessed us and given us great joy. We came to understand, that it did not say in

God's word to be thankful *for* all circumstances, but *in* all circumstances.

When you lose a child, there is a sorrow that can almost not be carried. At the same time, there is this sure knowledge of her being with God. So there is also joy. You learn to cry while laughing. and to smile while crying. That too is a gift from God.

God has blessed us in our retirement. He opened new doors for us. Allowed us to be part of great blessings and wonders in other countries and also back at home.

I can only say, "How richly God has dealt with us.: And yes, he is my best friend.

Andy's Journey

January 20th, 2014

Hello Family and friends, we are living with great uncertainty. I just got home and Andy is in the hospital. . Nothing is proven, nothing is clear at the moment. The reason he is in the hospital, is simply, so they can fast track him for all kinds of tests. MRI Cat scan of the brain, heart and liver. Bone scan of his whole body, etc. etc. If he simply waited for all those appointments, it could be months before we have answers. Now it will be two days at the most. We covet your prayers and will keep you all up to date.

January 21st, 2014

Let us then approach the throne of grace with confidence, So that we may receive mercy and find grace to help us in our time of need Hebrews 4:16

January 22nd, 2014

Not much of an update for today. He had a scan of his brain and liver. An MRI/bone scan and waiting for some more scans tomorrow. He is in good spirits. Remaining steadfast, trusting in our God.

January 23rd, 2014 (1)

No matter what happens today. This is the day that the Lord has made.

January 23rd, 2014 (2)

A native woman (Maria) was placed in Andy's room, just yesterday. Three other room mates, had complained about her presence in their rooms. Andy right away reassured her, he would have no problems sharing a room with her. Should I be worried? Anyway, she makes a loud sound trying to breath. Andy told her he simply takes out his hearing aids at night and will not hear her. Poor woman. Trying to think of what psalm to read with her and Andy today. Maybe ask her to pick the psalm, or will choose PS 23. Please keep us all in your prayers.

January 23rd, 2014 (3)

"David slayed his Goliath by focusing on God, instead of Goliath", a very important thing to remember in all our struggles and challenges in life.

January 23rd, 2014 (4)

We still do not know. An MRI was ordered for this morning, then cancelled. Now a PET scan is ordered and he will be transferred to University Hospital for that one. Andy is in good spirits. I was greeted by two sets of smiles. Andy and Maria, both were happy that Andy had slept and that there had been no complains about her trying to live. Sigh. But she did inform me, that he woke her up, cause he farted. And then both of them laughed out loud. Was pleased and privileged to be able to read God's word with her. She asked for Psalm 98. for it was about praising God. She also asked me to sing How great thou art, for it is her favorite song. I declined, because singing for me, would bring tears, right now, but if any of you want to go visit Andy, tonight. Please sing this song.

January 24th, 2014 (1)

So what do you think, my friends. Andy got bored, after I left. So he started walking around the hospital and found that the plants needed water so he watered them. Should I bring him a pail of dirt and a small shovel, so he can re-pot some of them?

January 24th, 2014 (2)

Back home again. Tomorrow they will have a look at his esophagus and take a biopsy. The PET scan has been scheduled for Jan. 29th at the U of A. He is in the Royal Alex and would love some visitors. No other news. Thank you for all your messages and prayers.

January 24th, 2014 (3)

"They will soar on wings like eagles; they will run and not grow weary, they will walk and not be faint." (Isaiah 40:30-31)
Hope in the Lord.
Hope in the Lord.

Hope in the Lord.

January 25th, 2014 (1)

Thankful for my children. Thankful for giving me a ride up to the hospital and back home every day. and thankful for filling up my car and being there for me.

January 25th, 2014 (2)

Well folks, the bone scan showed something on his fifth rib. Something on the bottom of his left lung, 3 cyst on his liver. Lung is fine. Cysts are benign. Brain scan was also all OK. Now the biopsy they took today yet and the PET scan will tell us more about the rib. We have a God of Miracles. God is Good.

January 25th, 2014 (3)

Andy had some tests done and Maria also had some procedure done. Both were a bit out of it. Andy was thrilled with all the visitors today and Maria also got visitors. I had given her a Little Warriors doll. Because she never had a childhood. She held the doll all day. When I left tonight, with Sylvia and the girls, she suddenly grabbed my hand and asked me to stay and pray with her. I told her I will pray for her tonight and pray with her tomorrow and followed my ride (Sylvia) out. Felt bad and good at the same time. Grateful to be in my shoes and not in hers. Grateful for good news about Andy. Maria is suffering and I am only asked to pray. Thankful, oh so thankful.

January 26th, 2014 (1)

"For I know the plans I have for you," declares the LORD, "plans to prosper you and not to harm you, plans to give you hope and a future." (Jeremiah 29:11)

January 26th, 2014 (2)

Today, the pastor's son came in for a visit. He read psalm 46 and prayed with Andy and Maria. Thank you so very much Joel. Proud to have you as friend. Also a big Thank you to Marian and Gerald for helping out today and for being a true brother and sister in Christ.

January 29th, 2014

So yesterday I woke up to a bout of Ménière's Disease. Had to go to the bathroom, so crawled there. Then back in bed. The phone ran a lot, but I simply could not get to it. I knew where my meds were, but could not get to that either. Hetty stopped by, to give me a ride to the hospital. Instead she fetched my meds, called Trixie and got my walking stick out of the motor home. Thank you so much friend. Jolene, came and heated up some soup for me and Trixie showed up with stew and two girls. They cleaned my house. THANK YOU SO MUCH! This morning I can see better and walk with my walking stick. Taking a shower was kind of scary, but I managed. Then came the call that I could pick up Andy. Trixie will do this. Again thank you all. Suddenly it is all about me. I had not had a bout for some 4 years. Hopefully I will get to know, what course of action we will need to take with Andy. More time to spend with my husband. Thank you all for your prayers and God Bless.

January 30th, 2014

"My grace is sufficient for you, for my power is made perfect in weakness." (2 Corinthians 12:9)

January 31st, 2014

Yes, our plate is full. Knowing that I have a Savior, who will carry this for us, is overwhelming..

February 1st, 2014

"Since, then, you have been raised with Christ, set your hearts on things above, where Christ is, seated at the right hand of God. Set your minds on things above, not on earthly things. For you died, and your life is now hidden with Christ in God." (Colossians 3:1-3)

February 5th, 2014

"Whoever dwells in the shelter of the Most High, will rest in the shadow of the Almighty. I will say of the lord, "He is my refuge and my fortress, my God, in whom I trust." (Psalm 91:1-2)

February 7th, 2014

Praying for a miracle.
We have known this for a couple of days.
There simply is no easy way to tell you.

Andy has cancer.

The cancer has spread to his hip bone rib and liver. It started in the esophagus entrance to the stomach. Radiation treatment will start soon and last for 10 days.

After that Chemo.

He has no pain, but is starting to have problems swallowing food. Not every day and just certain foods.

He is in good spirits, trusting in God's will for his life.

"In my Father's house are many mansions: if it were not so, I would have told you. I go to prepare a place for you." (John 14:2)

February 10th, 2014

I am making up a mass e-mail list, for updates on Andy. I will also continue to update on FB. Forgive me, if I miss anyone. We certainly appreciate the posts and emails. Over 100 per day. Forgive me, if I do not answer all of them. We do read all of them. Andy will start Radiation on the 13th. and will be going to the Cross Cancer clinic, daily, for 10 days. He will only be there for one hour a day, tops. He is still pain free, but eating does not always go to well. I just put on a big pan of chicken vegetable soup. That should work much better. Visitors are always welcome. (Not if you have a cold, please) He feels good, actually. I feel strangely tired, but am over my bout of Meniere Disease.

Yes, we are still praying for a miracle, for we have an almighty God. For what is in life and death our only aid? Our comfort when we are in trouble? This was our reading for today. We read it and both cried. Yet dear friends, it is all good.

February 11ᵗʰ, 2014

Great is Your faithfulness.

February 13ᵗʰ, 2014

We have just returned from the Cross Cancer Hospital. Andy received his first radiation treatment and we have a daily schedule till Feb 27ᵗʰ. He feels fine. No nausea just yet.

Still hoping and praying for a miracle, but resting in God's will for our lives.

February 14ᵗʰ, 2014

Of course I got flowers. It did bring tears to my eyes. I have a husband who buys me flowers at least 20 times a year. Love this man. Happy Valentine's day everyone!

We both cried, knowing this would be the last time he would buy flowers for this occasion.

Now for the second treatment.

Second treatment all done. Back home and doing well. A little tired. God is Good

February 15ᵗʰ, 2014

Psalm 121.

Horrible, horrible pain came during the night. He cried out for God to please take him now and I asked for the same thing. Never have I watched pain like this before. The Tylenol extra, Advil and Motrin, we had in our house, was not even making the slightest dent in it.

Thankfully Adrian took us to the hospital in Devon and he got some real painkillers.

Then, finally PAIN free! PTL. 20 hours in pain. He just had some soup and is smiling! Thank you all for your kind words and prayers.

February 16ᵗʰ, 2014

This is the day that the Lord has made. I will rejoice and be glad in it.

Not a restful night. Pain flared up and stayed around for a couple of hours. Will set up something, in order to wake every two hours and get some meds in my beloved. He is sleeping now. Praise God from whom all Blessings flow.

February 17ᵗʰ, 2014 (1)

Set the alarm for 1, 3 and 5 AM to administer medication. I woke up each time before the alarm went. Pain free night. Comfort, comfort, yea my people.

February 17ᵗʰ, 2014 (2)

Thankful for the family and friends who have offered and are now driving us for our appointments at the Cross Cancer Inst. Noticed that our nephew John, is coming all the way from Ontario, to do just that. THANKS!

February 19ᵗʰ, 2014

4 treatments down and 6 to go. So thankful, he has found some pain relief. The radiation to the hip was simply

the worst. Pain management was something new for us. It means 2 tablets, wait 3 hours and then 2 Advil and wait 2 hours. So this also means 3 times during the night. It sort of turned us into zombies for the day. This lasted from Saturday till yesterday afternoon. Now almost 6 hours between, it flares up again. Got 6 hours sleep, without needing to get up, last night. So thankful for drivers to the hospital and caring friends. I thought meals would not be a problem for me, but I wind up being oh so thankful for soup, baking and a meal dropped off at our house. He keeps most of everything down, as long as he has no hard crunchier food. That seems to get stuck in his esophagus. Today and yesterday, the radiation was to his stomach and nausea was expected, but did not happen. Thankful, oh so thankful.

Sometimes I feel like Peter walking on the water. So strong and sure of my faith, but then I look down and see the danger and I start to sink. But Jesus, He reaches out his hand … …

February 20th, 2014

"Create in me a clean heart, O God; and renew a right spirit within me." (Psalm 51:10)

February 21st, 2014

Radiation number 6 is now behind us. 4 More to go. The extreme pain comes from radiation to the bone. It makes the bone expand and the pain is extreme. Slowly but surely it is becoming less painful. No more bone radiations, just the stomach and esophagus. We again managed almost 5 hours of sleep, without waking up for pain relief.

Today we had our consultation with the Dr. A new one. She was truly nice and caring. After the radiation, we will wait 5 or 6 weeks, then a scan to see what help or damage, the radiation has done. Only then, will we need to decide to try Chemo. There is no cure. Only God can cure this cancer. "In you, Lord, I have taken refuge; let me never be put to shame. In your righteousness, rescue me and deliver me; turn your ear to me and save me. Be my rock of refuge, to which I can always go; give the command to save me, for you are my rock and my fortress." (Psalm 71: 1-3)

February 26th, 2014

2 More Radiation treatments to go. The pain is mostly gone and we now sleep through the night again.

He is starting to lose weight. 9 pounds, to date. He is still in very good spirits and was so happy to see his nephew, John Thanks John. God Bless you.

We have several people driving us to the Cross Cancer institute and I am so thankful for that.

Living in thankfulness for all God has given us and still gives us daily.

February 27th, 2014 (1)

"All the days are ordained for me were written in your book before one of them came to be." (Psalm 139:16)

February 27th, 2014 (2)

Done with Radiation treatments. Now a 5 or 6 week wait. Praise God.

A big THANK YOU to all who drove Andy to the Cancer clinic and back home.

February 28th, 2014

"For great is your love, reaching to the heavens; your faithfulness reaches to the skies." (Psalm 57:10)

Thank you to all who replied. I simply do not have time to reply to all of you, so just this THANK YOU will hopefully do for now. I read all of them to Andy.

Thank you also for the cards mailed to him/us. He loves receiving mail.

March 2nd, 2014

Hello Family and friends.

Yes, Thursday was the last treatment. Andy felt just fine and eager to start working on getting healthier. He slept well and we planned to go to PICS, the school most of our grandchildren attend for the concert and desert evening,

But, Friday started bad. Breakfast would not go down and he felt so weak. He did eat a little soup for lunch and I made him an omelet for supper. With sweet peppers, mushrooms, onions and sliced meatballs. He ate half of it and went back to bed. He also started to have pain again. Now in his stomach and was so tired. It is not nausea, it simply gets stuck, and there is some sort of obstruction.

Saturday was somewhat better. Ate breakfast and it stayed down. Soup for lunch and that also stayed down. Friends dropped in and brought a meal. Again it stayed down. He eats way, way less then he used to do and is now down 14 pounds. My skinny man is getting skinnier. He felt good and planned on going to Church on Sunday.

Sunday came and he woke up in pain. We switched from Advil to Tylenol extra strength and it helped dull the pain.

We listened on line to a service in Langley Church.

Unfortunately the computer quit and would not work for about 15 minutes, so we missed most of it.

Still we talked, prayed puzzled and laughed.

We listened to a sermon on Psalm 23. Very good and encouraging. We never walk alone, do we.

Andy is so thankful for this time together and looking forward to more, a visit from his sister and her husband from Ontario.

Take care and God Bless.

"For we know that if the earthly tent we live in is destroyed, we have a building from God, an eternal house in heaven, not built by human hands. Meanwhile we groan, longing to be clothed instead with our heavenly dwelling, because when we are clothed, we will not be found naked. For while we are in this tent, we groan and are burdened, because we do not wish to be unclothed but to be clothed instead with our heavenly dwelling, so that what is mortal may be swallowed up by life. Now the one who has fashioned us for this very purpose is God, who has given us the Spirit as a deposit, guaranteeing what is to come." (2 Corinthians 5: 1-5)

March 3rd, 2014

"Great is Thy faithfulness, O God my Father!
There is no shadow of turning with Thee;

Thou changest not, Thy compassions, they fail not:
As Thou hast been Thou forever wilt be.

"Summer and winter, and springtime and
harvest,
Sun, moon and stars in their courses above,
Join with all nature in manifold witness to
Thy great faithfulness, mercy and love.

"Pardon for sin and a peace that endureth,
Thine own dear presence to cheer and to guide,
Strength for today and bright hope for
tomorrow-
blessings all mine with ten thousand beside!

CHORUS:

Great is thy faithfulness, Great is Thy
faithfulness,
morning by morning new mercies I see;
All I have needed Thy grace has provided—
Great is Thy faithfulness, Lord, unto me!"

March 7th, 2014

"Let me hear joy and gladness; let the bones you broke
rejoice." (Psalm 51: 8)

March 8th, 2014

Hello Family and friends.

It seems to go from bad the one day, to somewhat good the next.

Eating became more and more a problem. Last Saturday was the last meal that stayed down. Andy always ate 3 fruits a day and that eating an orange became too painful, did not surprise me at all, but a banana. By Tuesday all fruit was stopped, all because of the extreme pain. Foods became more and more of a problem, but soup was still ok. So he ate some soup on Monday and Tuesday. Both bad days, pain wise. Now in his esophagus. The hip pain is totally gone.

By Thursday he was down to eating about 300 calories per day. Hot drinks hurt. Cold drinks hurt.

Friday morning, I made a high protein shake for him, again he could not drink it, so I put it 20 seconds in the microwave and gave him a straw to drink it with. It worked!

So we now make everything luke-warm. Ensure, booster and whatever I make myself, for him. I have him up to 1100 calories a day again and he looks better, with less pain. He can no longer tolerate calcium and Vit C. Potassium Vit. E, D and one other one, do go down. Drinks luke-warm coffee now. He used to drink it so hot.

So Friday was a good day. He felt much better all day. Same today. We had people stopping in and Andy loved it. and more came this afternoon and he is not even tired yet. 700 calories down and 500 more to go for today.

April 3 is scheduled for scans and CT test. April 10 will be a meeting with the Drs. day.

Please continue to keep us in your prayers.

Praise God from whom all Blessings flow.

Andy and Gerda

March 9th, 2014

Today, we, both Andy and I, made it to Church.

To top it all off, our grandson, sat and worshipped with us. Of course, I made the mistake of slipping Andy a peppermint. He sucked it and was suddenly engulfed in pain. What was I thinking? Austin went along for a coffee. It had been some years, since one of our daughters children came to see us.

Thankful for today.

March 10th, 2014

Thankful for what was posted in our bulletin.

"Andy has regularly endured pain, and has trouble swallowing food at times; he has lost weight also. He does not know what the Lord has in store for him, but he is at peace about going home to be with His Lord. Yet, the road is difficult and painful for him, for Gerda, and for his children. It is especially hard for the grandchildren. Please remember them. May the Holy Spirit counsel and comfort you all."

This does not mean that we no longer pray for a miracle.

March 10th 2014

Hello fam and friends.

Konnie and Ann have arrived and Andy is so very pleased with this visit. He loves having people over. Also every day 1 or 2 cards arrive. He does not know that I posted our address and I am not letting him know. Secrets between husband and wife.

Last Thursday Andy was still so weak, but he had taken in 1100 calories, so when we got visitors, he did talk and smile and was happy. Needed a sleeping pill to sleep, but did sleep. By Sunday he was good enough to attend a Church service, like I mentioned before.

If you had seen him last Wednesday, you would have thought he would not last much longer. I, myself, was ready to have him taken to the hospital and put on intravenous.

Well, yesterday he ate lasagna. (Thank you Tania) HE ATE A MEAL WITH US! We are overjoyed. He does not even look sick anymore. Still drinking the smoothies, but also other foods. It seems the radiation to his esophagus, that caused all this pain, is healing and thankfully it is allowing food to pass through. Nothing bulky or crunchy yet, but solid food. His dizziness has also gone. Thank you for all your prayers. No he is not healed. He still has terminal cancer, but we are thankful to our God and Father for this reprieve.

God be with you all.

March 12th, 2014

"And let us run with perseverance the race marked out for us, fixing our eyes on Jesus, the pioneer and perfecter of faith. For the joy set before him he endured the cross, scorning its shame, and sat down at the right hand of the throne of God. Consider him who endured such opposition from sinners, so that you will not grow weary and lose heart.: (Hebrews 12: 1b-3)

March 16ᵗʰ, 2014

"Count it all joy, my brothers, when you meet trials of various kinds, for you know that the testing of your faith produces steadfastness. And let steadfastness have its full effect, that you may be perfect and complete, lacking in nothing. If any of you lacks wisdom, let him ask God, who gives generously to all without reproach, and it will be given him. But let him ask in faith, with no doubting, for the one who doubts is like a wave of the sea that is driven and tossed by the wind." (James 1: 2-7)

March 22ⁿᵈ, 2014

Hello family and friends.

What a difference a week makes. He was still so weak when Konnie and Ann came, but every day was better. By Friday he was eating everything and only took one Advil. No more narcotics. Then on Saturday Konnie and Ann took us out to a Chinese restaurant. He surprised all of us with the amount of food he ate. On Sunday, we went to church twice and had a get together with other family members at night. A long day, but he did it.

He has lost a total of 19 or 20 pounds, but it is now on the upswing. He has gained a pound! This is just a small house and those pounds had to go someplace, so yes they are now firmly entrenched on my hips. Stress eating. I know. I know. No advise please.

He is still also drinking energy drinks to boost his weight. Sleeping much better and happy to be eating. Kidneys are sort of sluggish now, but drinking cranberry juice seems to help. He has had this before, so we take the same action as always and will contact the Dr. if it persist.

We had an evaluation done, or rather our house did, for palliative care. The house passed with flying colors. Thanks Adrian!

Devon Hospital called us, to inform us we could pick up a chair for the shower. He had had a couple of dizzy spells and was afraid to take a shower. This old lady could also not keep him up, so this is the solution for now. It is "peace of mind" for me, even if right now he does not need to use it. Unexpectedly, my tears flowed, when I looked at the contraption in our shower. But yes, still thankful for those small items.

Meals and soup were dropped off at our place. Even if I had said I could manage, I am overwhelmed with thankfulness for these tokens of love and communion of Saints.

Konnie and Ann left us on Monday and Andy drove them to the airport. Who would have thought …

Yesterday Gerrie and Bauke arrived. So happy to see them. They will be here for the weekend, returning Monday.

Jannie and Corrie will arrive Tuesday the 25th and stay the week. Andy is so looking forward to seeing his sisters and I am thankful he feels great again.

Still taking every thing by the day. Trusting and relying on God, our Father.

"Do not be anxious about anything, but in everything by prayer and supplication with thanksgiving let your requests be made known to God. And my God will supply every need of yours according to his riches in glory in Christ Jesus." (Philippians 4: 6-7)

How much, much more, this verse now means to us.

Take care and God Bless.

Andy and Gerda

March 29th, 2014

Dear Family and friends.

Not much to report this time.

He had a good week and was happy with the visit of his "little" sisters Corrie and Jannie.

He also gained 5 pounds, so thankful for that. He needed to get his strength back. Only problem is, that now that he is gaining, I should be losing. Not so. Rats!

Only one night of pain. Kidneys this time. So more painkillers and a salve to put on his back. It seemed to work. Also sleep tablets are now needed. I took some too. Sometimes I am more tired than he is.

We had a lead on a free Hospital bed, but the wrong information was passed on to us, and we lucked out. It simply was not to be and thankfully we do not need it yet.

Looking forward to 2 more visitors on Monday, Christine and Cora and happy that we, ourselves can go and pick them up from the airport. They will be here till April 3rd, That is also the day for his next two scans.

April 4th, New visitors will arrive "Gerrie and Joanne" and by April 10, the day that those two will be leaving, we should have the results of the scans and the meeting with the doctors.

He loves all the cards you have sent. A big thank you to all.

Till then, God Bless and take care.

It is well, it is well, with my soul.

Andy and Gerda

March 31st, 2014

"I will praise the LORD as long as I live; I will sing praises to my God while I have my being." (Psalm 146:2)

Christine and Cora left us this morning. Great people. Great visit. Great time. Andy is doing very well and we do appreciate those visits so much.

Tomorrow Joanne and Gerrie. Now to the Cross Cancer for 2 more scans.

We feel so Blessed

April 3rd, 2014 (1)

We will not know the result of the scan till April 10th. Thank you for your prayers.

April 3rd, 2014 (2)

The miracle might not be what you expected. Remember that.

April 4th, 2014

Gerrie and Joanne have arrived! Let the games begin!

April 5th, 2014

Dear Fam and friends.

Andy is getting stronger every day. He is eating well and enjoying the visitors. This week we first had "Christine and Cora" and now "Gerrie and Joanne" are here.

Yes, they are working on "The Puzzle"

Andy has gained 2 more pounds and started cleaning up the damaged greenhouse. We are planning a trip to Red Deer, to visit Joanne's sis in law. Andy driving. Who would have thought. God is good. Of course there are 2 more people with a valid drivers license, so no worries.

We had the scan done on April 3rd and on the 10th we will have a meeting with the doctors, to see if any other action should be taken.

Still more cards are arriving and he is so pleased with them.

It is warming up. The sun is shining and hopefully we soon will see the grass and new growth.

Every day is a gift from God. We thank our Father who has planted faith in our hearts and we thank Him for every day he gives us.

Happy that things are going OK for us. Andy is of good cheer, but … … we have our moments. It has been constantly busy. Constantly visitors. I so appreciate that they are here. Thankfully they either sleep at Sylvia's or Trixie's. And all have taken us out for supper. Still lots of baking being dropped off.

April 7th, 2014

I made sure it was spring today and will slowly but surely move forward and become summer. I hung the laundry on the line, OUTSIDE! Only a little pile of snow to climb over. I love to go a wandering. Come on folks, sing along with me … … … … … … …

April 8th, 2014

"But for you who revere My name, the sun of righteousness will rise with healing in its rays." (Malachi 4:2)

April 10th, 2014

Hello friends and family.

Update on Andy.

Well we had our follow-up after the scan.

Nice doctor. She was very clear and calm. Told us that it did not look any better and that the cancer had spread some more. Some spots on the lungs and glands are infected. The tumors in the liver have grown.

So we had to decide, if we wanted to try Chemo. Not because there is a possible cure, but to strictly prolong his life. Without Chemo, he will have 4 to 6 months to live. With Chemo 6 month to a year. Of course this is humanly speaking.

We have a merciful, loving God, who knows the path we have to walk. He will continue to walk with us on this final journey, as He has walked with us all the days of our life.

Andy is feeling great. He is taking down our little greenhouse and will be moving it to Trixie's place. She is the other gardener in the family. He has gained 9 pounds back, of the 20 he lost. No pain, sleeping and eating well. He simply does no longer look like a sick man. Happy and thankful for this gift.

Joanne and her mom, Andy's sister Gerrie, have left for Ontario. It was so nice to have them over and so nice to get to know Joanne again.

We surely appreciated all those who came to visit. Thankful we could enjoy it. Laugh, talk and have fun.

In Christ alone.

April 11th, 2014

We went to Chemo 'school' today. Learned a lot and have a lot more to learn. First Chemo, starts on the 15th of April. 7 am!

We are good, truly. And yes, sometimes we just hold onto each other and simply cry.

April 14th, 2014

Nice visit with Jane, Lori and Marrisa. Thank you for the Boterkoek and the bread.

April 15th, 2014

We are home again. All day at the Cross Cancer institute. First Chemo treatment behind us. Feeling sleepy, tired etc. But then we had to be up by 5.30 and just got home.

April 17th, 2014

God is NOT dead. Yes we saw the movie tonight. It was certainly worth it. We sat nearly up in the front, as much away from others as we possibly could. He, Andy, wanted to go and see it, so we did. Andrew and Jesse also came and saw the movie with us. God is good.

April 19th, 2014 (1)

Who wants to join us for supper at a Chinese restaurant. Buffet preferred. Andy want to hold on to our habit that simply seems livelong, of going out for a meal every Saturday evening. Saturday has always been our date night. Love this man.

April 19th, 2014 (2)

Hello family and friends.

This week has been such a good week. Andy laughing, talking, eating and gaining weight.

Tuesday was the first chemo day and we had to be at the hospital by 7 am, so getting up at 5 am.

First blood work. Then an appointment with the Dr.J. We quickly got something to eat, after that meeting and at 12 noon the chemo began. He fell asleep twice and I read or walked around. We picked up KFC on the way back home and all was well.

For the rest of the week, all went well. We had visitors, We listened to a couple of good sermons, That was from a minister we will be considering calling.

On Good Friday we went to Church and then for lunch to Montana rest., with Dwayne, Trix and their children.

Today we had Rick and Liz from BC, they came to visit their daughter Annemarie. We had a good visit. They stayed for lunch and it was so good to see them again.

Andy just loves Chinese food and wanted to go out for supper. We did and again he ate well. He has gained about 11 pounds back, from the 20 he had lost.

As we drove home, he suddenly said he was so tired. Just like that.

We came home and he drank 1/3 rd of a cup of coffee. Sat very quietly in his chair and again told me how tired he was.

By 8.30 he was in bed. Almost too tired to undress. So tired, it brought him and me to tears.

His temp is slowly going up. I will have to keep an eye on this during the night.

Yes, God is Good. He is with us, as we walk this walk. That does not mean we have no tears. No sorrow. It also does not mean we have no hope. No hope for a miracle. We know we have an Almighty God. An all knowing, loving God.

And we know: HE has risen!

Trusting in his faithfulness.

Andy and Gerda

April 20th, 2014

Because He lives, I can face tomorrow

April 21st, 2014

Last night, we had a nice visit from Connie and Billy. Then the pain set in. The Dr. had given us a prescription of Tylenol 3 but all the info sheets that came with his Chemo meds said, not to take Tylenol. Spend an hour on the phone with an emerge nurse. Glad they have so much patience. I had to check Andy for several things. His temp was also creeping up. So I needed to monitor this till about 2 am. On the lighter side, I got a lot done on the latest puzzle. Tonight we watched the band on live stream, Winnipeg. It was certainly worth the watching. Andy took only 1 Advil today and food stayed in. I think I should turn in too. Night friends. Take care and God Bless.

April 23rd, 2014

Who wants to come for coffee? No colds or sniffles, of course. Visiting hours are from 10-12 and 2-4.

April 25th, 2014

Thanking God, for the people who make life more joyful, for us and many others.

April 26th, 2014 (1)

To all of you who would like a more happy, content and peaceful life. Every single morning, spend 15 minutes reading, praying and meditating with God. Unless you are simply too busy, then you should spend 30 minutes.

April 26th, 2014 (2)

Hello Fam and friends.

Not much to report.

Andy is very tired. He has had bouts of nausea and also pain. This pain sets in about 2 hours after the chemo pills are taken. We manage it with only 1 Advil, so not bad at all. He is again eating less, but still eating.

We have had some visitors, but it has, in general been a quiet week. Living, talking, reading, praying, laughing and yes, also some tears. He misses seeing the kids and grandkids, but there are so many illnesses going around, it is better this way. At least he can watch Adrian and Sylvia's kids. We thankfully have a lot of windows and seeing the kids always puts a smile on his face. He also enjoys watching the various birds on the birdfeeder.

This coming Monday, he will be 79 years old. So thankful. We simply cannot understand why people lie about their age, or do not want their age mentioned in the Church bulletin.

If you are thankful for every day God gives you, how can you lie about your age?

Next week we hope to welcome some more family, both from Ontario and BC.

What is in life and death your only aid? Yes, our comfort is in Him who gives us this comfort. This trust, that everything is in His Almighty hands.

Thankful for family and friends.

April 28th, 2014

Happy Birthday Andy! We hope you have a enjoyable day with family and friends!

April 30ᵗʰ, 2014

This could be our final day. God be with all those who mourn.

Great is Thy faithfulness.

May 1ˢᵗ, 2014

Today is National day of Prayer.

"So that with one mind and one voice you may glorify the God and Father of our Lord Jesus Christ." (Romans 15:6)

May 2ⁿᵈ, 2014

Nancy and Jean have arrived!

May 3ʳᵈ, 2014

Another week has flown by. We welcomed visitors from Ontario and BC. Hardly any pain, this week.

Getting used to the routine of meds, etc.

The latest thing is, that I am now married to Yul Brynner, for his hair is all gone. It was coming out by the handfuls and he pleaded with me to shave his head, so I did. He laughed, I cried, but only because that is what females do.

"Praise the Lord. Praise the Lord, my soul. I will praise the Lord all my life; I will sing praise to my God as long as I live. Do not put your trust in princes, in human beings, who cannot save. When their spirit departs, they return to the ground; on that very day their plans come to nothing. Blessed are those whose help is the God of Jacob, whose hope is in the Lord their God." (Psalm 146: 1-5)

Next week, check up Chemo treatment, etc.

Thanking you all for your prayerful support.

All our love, Andy and Gerda

May 5th, 2014

Len, Gord, Nancy and Jean came to visit. We had such a great visit with them. Short, but oh so sweet. We all gathered at Adrian and Sylvia and sang our hearts out.

Thanks again for coming. Love you all. Safe travel and God Bless.

May 6th, 2014

Today's announcement! 6 More weeks till the longest day. After that the days will shorten and winter will be on it's way. BTW Andy just told me that. Can I hit him?

May 7th, 2014 (1)

So, May 6th we had to be at the hospital for blood work, check up and prep for May 7th Chemo treatment.

The Dr. reminded me about the pills he had to take one hour before Chemo and to get the other prescription filled. I dutiful said yes to everything. We had to be at the Cross at 9.30 and got out at 11 am. Not bad. Now to the nearest place for filling a prescription. Andy was tired so he sat in the store at a table, so I knew they must have food there. We had to wait the usual 30 minutes for the meds. I spotted a Timmies, so coffee, bagel and soup, for the two of us.

The check-up had shown that Andy lost another 5 pounds, so I most likely gained that weight.

Home at 1 pm. I knew I better do some laundry, or quit taking showers. So I got to work. Dryer and washer going full blast, so no use trying to talk. Thankfully I could simply take a prepared meal out of the freezer. Thank you Marj.

The test had shown that Andy did not drink the required amount of daily water. So hard to keep track. I fill a container with water and that is what he has to drink every day. Nice and cold, right out of the fridge. With visitors, it also winds up on the table for drinking water for all of us, and that is where I missed some of the right amounts to refill. At least Andy is now also taking this seriously and is over his "Oh well" attitude.

At supper I gave him the last of this round of Chemo pills and set out the meds he had to take in the morning.

BIG SHOCK! The 2 different little pills he had to take the morning of May 7th, I gave him the morning of April 18th. Now what? Too late to phone the Cross. Help line does not give prescriptions. So off to Devon Hosp. to find a dr, willing to prescribe 2 different tablets for just one day.

Andy was so tired by now, he asked me to drive. I know that was even more tiring, for he had to point out every pothole, stop sign, stoplight, speed limit, etc. etc.

I had all the papers, etc. with me, so I could show the Dr. the mistake I made.

Only 3 people ahead of us. Then they first had to prod, poke and take Andy's blood pressure. Out a bracelet on him, so that they would not give him to the wrong mother, I guess. Wait again.

Finally, it was our turn. I explained. He said: "No problem" and out we walked with the prescription. Both so tired.

Andy now wanted to drive. Less stress then telling his wife how to, lol. Shoppers drugs was open. Andy stayed in the car, while I went to get it filled. No chair to sit down and no wall to lean against. I did eye some display cases, but was afraid they would come crashing down, if I tried to lean against them. Wandered around the store, wondering how anyone could think they could buy food here, except for dairy products. Yes, lots of pictures of food, but food with a 3 point sermon on the side, cannot be food. No food, till I came eye to eye with a 50% off chocolate bunny. Almost bought it because by now I wanted to bite some one's head off. Did not buy it. After all I had to spend extra for meds, I misused. Could have bought it from the money we saved, by Andy no longer needing shampoo. LOL.

Somehow we made it home. Andy went straight to bed. I folded the rest of the laundry and boiled eggs for egg salad sandwiches. We decided to bring food for Chemo day. Gathered some books and bottled water and will be better prepared than the last time.

May 7th, 2014 (2)

Woke up at 5 am and stayed awake. That is what happens when you take a sleeping pill and go to bed 2 hours earlier than usual. Took a shower, checked FB, of course. Made coffee and finally woke up Andy. He took a shower and made a discovery. No more need for a hairbrush!

Chemo for the day is over. 5 hours in total at the hospital. I am told that is not bad at all.

Picked up some more Anti-nausea meds. Lots more of Chemo pills 8 or 10 per day. Will have to real it all over very carefully. I found out that I had not done anything wrong after all. They simply kept them at the pharmacy for pick up 3 weeks later. We should have been told. Oh well. Now we know that we have to pick up pre Chemo pills on May 23rd. I drove this morning. Heavy traffic. Almost did not make it on time. Dropped Andy at the front door and then went and parked. Great Hospital. Excellent service, even if it means administering Chemo to Andy. Glad we took egg salad sandwiches with us. They come around serving coffee, etc., to all of us. Andy made friends with the guy in the next chair, that sure speeds up the time.

Thankful to our Heavenly father for giving us each day.

Thankful for a cheerful, thankful, husband.

Unto the Hills I lift my voice.

May 10th, 2014

Dear friends and Family.

The first two days after Chemo are the hardest. Well we sure found out. Andy was so very tired, the Chemo day and the day after Chemo. He did not eat much, nor drink enough and spend a lot of time running to the bathroom.

In fact he felt so sick, he feared he would not even make it till Mother's day. So he told me he had flowers for me, but they were hidden in a cool place in the shop. Love that man. To be sure and go looking for them on Sunday.

The second day, he felt much better. Even whistling. Worked outside for about one hour and then came in. We had a much appreciated visit with Darlene and her kiddos. He had had some cereal for breakfast and it stayed in.

Lunch simply would not. He tried drinking water, but was so nauseated, he could no longer do it. Soup would not go down. The bathroom became his hangout for the late afternoon and he was getting weaker. I have to record everything and decided to get on the phone and ask if I should take him in to the hospital, for I know he was getting dehydrated. They said, "Yes, take him to the nearest hospital." What a difference IV makes!

I left him at the hospital, after they had him all hooked up, blood taken and then he was taken for x-rays.

I cannot drive in the dark, so needed to go home. Adrian and Sylvia, picked him up around 11. Thank you from the bottom of my heart.

This morning he discovered some small ulcers in his mouth. That also is expected. Hope he will be able to eat and drink. No pain, so that is a Blessing.

Sometimes I simply cannot believe in the Miracle we pray for. I know God answers prayers, but we must also remember, He answers prayers for the furtherance of the Kingdom. His will be done, can become the hardest prayer. For we so badly want our will to be done.

Psalm 121, Unto the Hills … … … … … …

Group hug.

May 11th, 2014

"Fear of the LORD is the beginning of knowledge. Only fools despise wisdom and discipline. Listen, my child, to what your father teaches you. Don't neglect your mother's teaching. What you learn from them will crown you with grace and clothe you with honor." (Proverbs 1: 7-9)

May 14th, 2014 (1)

"How precious also are Your thoughts to me, O God! How great is the sum of them! If I should count them, they would be more in number than the sand; When I awake, I am still with You." (Psalm 139:17-18)

May 14th, 2014 (2)

In Christ alone.

May 14th, 2014 (3)

Hello Fam and friends,

In my Fathers house are many mansions. This is what keeps going through my head. If it is not so, He would not have told us.

Day 3 started early.

He could not keep anything down and again we went to the hospital. It became a daily trip, with just the one time staying over in the hospital.

He so badly wanted to go and attend Church, but again it was not to be. Sunday evening was the 4th time in emergency. They asked me to bring him back the next day, in the afternoon, for one more litre.

It was a most difficult night, with him getting weaker and no longer being able to stand. Then his temp went up and up. By 5 am I called Adrian out of bed to help me get him in my car. This time I drove right up to the emergency doors. They opened and I drove right in, ran to get a nurse to help me get him in a wheel chair. This time they kept him there.

No more white blood cells. Potassium, calcium and magnesium, way down Blood 97/47

He also had a bad fall in the hospital. Thankfully no broken bones.

Has not had Chemo since last Friday, because nothing stays down

He is so tired. Not even able to walk. Too tired to talk. Hooked up to machines. I read psalm 23 to and for him. Prayed with him.

He is receiving all kinds of meds. He has a blood infection. He will go for an ultrasound in the morning. For this they have to take him to Leduc. There is also talk about transferring him to the Cross Cancer clinic.

When we left today, his blood was 103/51, So thankfully going up again. Still not eating. Just smiles at us.

He and we know, that our Redeemer lives.

Trusting in His faithfulness.

Gerda

May 16th, 2014

Hello to all my in laws friends and family. … Dad has a long road ahead of him if it is the Lord's will that he recover from his blood infection and the toll that it has taken on his body. The chemo. has striped his body of its immune system and other essentials that the body needs. They are giving him what they can and in increments that hopefully his body will not reject. He is very weak. As of this morning he seems to be doing a bit better.. ... Fever has gone down and blood pressure is stabilizing. He sleeps most of the time with small periods of awake in between. My mother in law stayed with him at the hospital last night, but hopes to go home to sleep this evening. Thank you all for asking how they are doing.., we covet all your prayers. Sylvia

May 17th, 2014 (1)

I will be at Devon hospital. most likely, staying overnight. Thank you for all your prayers.

May 17th, 2014 (2)

"For the Lord God is a sun and shield; he bestows favor and honor. No good thing does the Lord withhold from those who walk uprightly." (Psalm 84:11)

Andy went to be with his Lord and Savior, on May 18th, 2014.

May 19th, 2014

Andy's funeral is Thursday at 1:00 in Immanuel. I will post the rest of the details as soon as we know more

Final Update on Andy

May 26th, 2014

This will be the hardest update of all.

Jan 20th, was the date when all this started. On the 28th, he was told, he had terminal cancer. They gave him 2 to 4 months to live.

And live he did. To the fullest. He opted for Radiation and Chemo, not for a cure, for at this stage only God could grant a cure. There was a chance of prolonged life. 6 to 12 months.

God granted him 4 months.

God also granted him the sure knowledge of salvation. He knew he was going to his Savior. Family and friends marveled at his disposition. Still the same Andy. Laughing, talking and working in his garden. He gave away many items and instructed me in the growing and handling of his tulips, lilies, Hyacinths daffodils, etc. etc. Told me when to have the oil changed in the car and marked on the calendar when I could expect the garbage pick-up. And he talked and worried about his grandkids. He longed to see them as often as he possibly could. Hungered for their affection and worried about them walking in God's way.

And most of all we grieved. And most of all we healed. I never knew what a blessing it is to know the time we have been allotted on the earth. the privilege to grieve together. To pray together. To plan together. To cry in each other's arms. To praise God for His faithfulness.

Yet, he was so thankful. So thankful for his, as he called it, amazing retirement years. The opportunities God had placed on his way. The joy of seeing faith in action. The smile on his face when he could hand a Bible to a person who simply hungered for the word of God. The joy when he saw the students in Timor, now attending a Christian school. He thanked God daily for having had this amazing gift. That dear friends, was our miracle.

The work in Indonesia goes on. So does the work in Cuba. Other faithful Godly servants have picked up the reigns.

He now rejoices, together with his beloved Peggy, before the throne of God.

For nothing, absolutely nothing, can separate us from the love of God.

"For I am convinced that neither death nor life, neither angels nor demons, neither the present nor the future, nor any powers, neither height nor depth, nor anything else in all creation, will be able to separate us from the love of God that is in Christ Jesus our Lord." (Romans 8: 38-39)

So dear family and friends, I will leave you with these words:

> "Rejoice in the Lord always. I will say it again: Rejoice! Let your gentleness be evident to all. The Lord is near. Do not be anxious about anything, but in every situation, by prayer

and petition, with thanksgiving, present your requests to God. And the peace of God, which transcends all understanding, will guard your hearts and your minds in Christ Jesus.

Finally, brothers and sisters, whatever is true, whatever is noble, whatever is right, whatever is pure, whatever is lovely, whatever is admirable—if anything is excellent or praiseworthy—think about such things. Whatever you have learned or received or heard from me, or seen in me—put it into practice. And the God of peace will be with you." (Philippians 4: 4-9)

Gerda Vandenhaak.

Eulogy

May 27th, 2014

Today, with his permission, I will share our son John's Eulogy:

On behalf of my family, I would like to thank you all for your condolences, your care and your friendship with my parents as well as with us. Every one of you is greatly appreciated. My Dad, Andrew Vandenhaak was a great Husband, Father, father in law, and Grandfather.

I could spend a lot of time telling stories of how my mom remembers him, how I remember him, how my brothers and sisters remember him, how the grandchildren remember him, how others remember him, and then we would be here for a very loooong time.

I am sure we all remember my dad as a man who loved to tell stories. His house was always open for visitors. I can hardly remember many Sundays, that dad and mom did not have company over, and dad always had many stories to tell and never ran out of things to talk about.

But more importantly dad loved the Lord, and always left us the example that there is nothing more important in this life than our lives as Christians. My dad was a truck driver for 37 years and a lot of that was long distance. I am proud to say that he retained a perfect ticket free driving record the entire time. He was often gone for overnight, but never once was he away on the weekends. No matter what he would either drive around the clock to be home Saturday night or he would refuse to take some trips but by Sunday he was always, always in church with his family.

My dad loved my mom, and left us the example that no matter what the marriage was for life and he remained faithful to her for the just over 52 years that they were married. He loved his children, and always wanted the best for them. That did not mean having the best job or making the most money. It meant remaining faithful to God. And I can thankfully say that though we all have our struggles and failures we are all trying to follow God in our lives He loved his grandchildren, and to the end of his life his greatest concern was for their spiritual wellbeing. When I first learned that dad had terminal cancer, I was a little shook up and phoned him as soon as possible. His first words to me were., "Don't worry about me, I know where I am going and I am ready" Then further in our conversation it became apparent that while he was ready to be united with Jesus, he did not like the idea of leaving his grandchildren behind. He had this concern for them. What if they don't understand. What if one of them choses to reject God.

Jesus has given all of us the offer of salvation and eternal life. What is our response to that? The bible teaches that to all who receive the gift of Jesus *he gives the right to become children of God. And if we have received that gift we had better be doing something with it. And it's never about how much we are doing, or what we are doing, or whether it's right or wrong way of doing it. It's about where is your heart, and why are you doing it. I want to say this to all my nieces and nephews, and my children of course. You know you can see grandpa again. As you are grieving and missing grandpa you are probably more eager to see him again than you are to spend eternity with Jesus. Jesus died for all of us, and we will not only be with Jesus for eternity, we will also be reunited with all of our loved ones. This is just an added benefit that God gives us. You need to follow Him. This was grandpa's greatest wish for all of you. Grandpa wants to see you all again. And here again I can thankfully say that all of you are being raised in Christ centered homes, and many of you are already serving him.*

Dad was always an energetic man. It is fair to say that he never really retired. He just slowed down a bit. When he stopped doing work that brought him income, he became involved in many different ministries. There he as well as mom, left a legacy for us to follow. An example that everyone should try to follow. After making a trip to Cuba they noticed a lack of bibles among the churches there as well as great poverty. God gave them a heart for the people there and over the last 13 years they made 37 trips to Cuba, helping 17 different churches, bringing over 1000 Bibles, as well as Christian books and supplies of all sorts to the people of Cuba. In addition to that they made three trips to Indonesia to visit with my cousin Mary- Lynn and her husband Yonson Dethan who pastors a church there. God gave them a heart for the people there as well and dad and mom worked relentlessly with Yonson and Mary-Lynn setting up Children of Light, which helps children and sets up Christian schools and raising support for the people there. They drove all over Canada sharing with churches about the work there. God greatly blessed this and today there are over 1500 students. Then while at home they still became involved in different local ministries as well. We were also blessed to have them come and join us in our ministry in Mexico for Christmas a year and a half ago.

Dad remained active right to the end. Still the last days that he was home with mom, he could be found outside working in the garden, or playing soccer with some grandkids. While staying in the hospital a few months ago for tests he noticed that the plants had not been watered, so he promptly got to work and began watering the plants in his hospital gown. Only three weeks ago he was at a friend's dairy farm, where he jumped over the fence. And just 8 days before he passed away, he was burning some garbage in the burning barrel, when a grass fire started, and then with the help of my daughter Alyson, he stomped out the fire.

In the last two months, dad enjoyed visits from his 4 sisters, two brothers in law and a sister in law, as well as several nieces and nephews. He will be missed by many.

While yes, this is a sad time here, as we will all miss him, it is a time of great rejoicing in heaven. Dad is now dancing and praising God. He is not only united with Jesus, but he is also reunited with my sister Peggy, and with all his other loved ones. That is something we can rejoice about. God is good, all the time.

As dad would always say to people in Cuba and Indonesia, when he left those places, now that he has left this world for a better place, he would have these same words to say to all of you here.

"God be with you till we meet again"

Thank you.

Sometimes

May 20th, 2014

Every once and a while, I go and reread all those supporting messages on face-book. I am completely overwhelmed by them and by all the snail mail. The donations to Word and Deed, in Andy's memory. Trista raising funds for Cancer research, in Andy's Memory. God Bless you all. Thank you from the bottom of my heart. As to how I feel?

Sometimes.

When in the early, very early morning.

I walk outside.

Coffee in hand.

Early sunshine rays on my face.

I stand there.

Looking at the trees, at the lawn.

And see nothing.

For my eyes are turned inwards.

Then tears come.

They run down my face and it surprises me.

They fall.

On my hands.

On the deck.

Not tears of sadness.

But they fall.

And fall.

Not tears of joy.
They fall.
Tears of healing.
Tears of cleansing.
A peace, beyond understanding.
And I feel the hand of God.
Yes.
The hand of God.
Great is your faithfulness

Camping: July 2014

Adrian, Sylvia, Dwayne, Trixie and twelve grandchildren had booked three sites at Herald provincial park in B.C. This was as a surprise for Andy and me. Andy did not make it, as we all know. I truly enjoyed it.

The boat.
The beach.
The sun.
The sand.
But in the silence of the night, I cry.

The fun.
The fire.
The love.
The laughter.
But in the silence of the night, I sigh.

The friends.
The food.
The hugs.
The hope.
But in the silence of the night, the why.

The children's children. Yes the generation,
Restore in me the joy of my salvation.
Yet, in the silence of the night, I cry.

Tears of sorrow.
Tears of loss.
Alone.
In Christ alone.
I dry my tears.
Lay down my fears.
In the silence of the night.

Amen.

Knock and it Will Be Opened

I stand at the door and I knock.
I knock again.
And again.
Don't you hear me LORD?
I told you what I want.
I told you what I need.
and I knock.
I hammer my fist at this door.
I cry.
I wail.
I whimper and sink down.
and down.
Disintegrated.
A heap.
On the floor.

I feel the sunlight on the back of my hand.
Sunlight?
Sun?
The door is closed.
How can this be?
I look.
Windows?
Three of them?
But Father, I did not ask for windows?
The door, Father.
Open the door!

Sitting up now.
Looking at the windows.
Not daring to look out.
Those are not the windows I would have picked.
Wrong make and model.

God gave me three windows.
Why, my Father. Why?

A window to LAUGH.
A window to LOVE.
A window to LIVE.
My Lord.
My Master.
My Savior.

January 13th, 2015

Last year at this time, I was sitting here writing my Facebook note '52 Years'. I was thankful and happy. We had no idea how our lives would change, just a couple of weeks later. It was to be our last anniversary together. God granted us time. Not only time to grieve, but also time to celebrate and to rejoice in the times we had together. Andy kept telling me how thankful he was, that he had been granted such an amazing retirement. He loved to serve, to give and to share. He was so thankful that his siblings and other family members came to tell him goodbye and Godspeed. He so trusted in his God and Father. He rejoiced in the children and grandchildren who came to visit and showed their love for him. I still live in thankfulness for the man God had chose to be my husband. Yes, being by myself has been hard. And yet, it has been good. We had just merged Children of Light with Word and Deed and had also made our last trip to Cuba as a couple. I have begged my God to give me purpose in life; to show me what He wants me to do. Like usual, His plans were different. While I looked at the closed door, He had opened windows all over the place. New people came into my life. New friendships have been formed. New purpose in life. Not what I was looking for, but it came with great joy and thankfulness. It has taken time, to find my trust in God. My refuge. My place of rest.

The Edge

I stand and I wonder.
I stand at the edge.
I don't want to go there.
But I am, on the very ledge.

Clawing, struggling, holding on
I do so not want to walk that road.
I have accepted that they are gone.
So why pick up that load?

The nice and smiling people,
Drive me to build a wall.
I don't want stinking thinking.
I don't want that at all.

My Lord and dearest Savior.
Keep me from caving in.
Pull me back from darkness,
That lays so deep within.

Help me to fight my demon,
Hovering to devour,
That ever roaring Lyon,
Is knocking at the door.

Unto the hills I lift my eyes,
When troubled or afraid.
Knowing You are with me,
and will come to my aid.

Like hinds' feet in high places
I soar into the light.
Yes, You are always with me.
E'en in the darkest night.

My Master.
My Lord.
My Savior.

Final Words

I have completed the rough draft of my 'book'. There's only about one hundred pages.

Today, I worked on *Andy's Journey;* the hardest part of all.

I am mostly writing this little book for my children and grandchildren, so they might remember their Grandpa and me. But moreover, I hope that it will give them the courage and will to keep on going when life throws you a curve ball. I hope it somehow will make them laugh and cry and also teach them compassion, understanding, caring and empathy. I hope that it will help them to understand that indeed, one person can make a difference. And to keep on going on when no one believes in you; to encourage them.

Should others read this book, then I hope and pray that this little book will also encourage them on their journey through life.

Above all, may you all live in thankfulness to our God and Father.

Gerda Vandenhaak nee Blokhuis

Printed in the United States
By Bookmasters